introduction

THE INCLEMENT WEATHER ONE RAW SPRING EVENING PRESENTED TWO OPTIONS. I could bunker in, or I could venture out and take advantage of the empty seats at one of the local restaurants. I chose the latter course and decided on Chuko, a ramen shop about a half-mile walk from my apartment. I soldiered into the gusty, wet wind, taking note of the empty restaurants, where hosts and servers stood somberly among empty tables.

At Chuko, though, the windows were clouded over with steam, as diners bent over piping hot bowls of ramen, slurping up noodles. When my vegetarian ramen arrived, it was everything I'd been hoping for: a rich, cloudy miso-based broth engulfing a tangle of tender noodles, topped with a scattering of sweet cabbage, chunks of squash, and an egg so soft it became one with the broth when I poked it open with my chopstick. I felt so pleased with myself, so rewarded for having endured the miserable weather. I looked around the restaurant and saw the same satisfaction on the other diners' faces. Storm? What storm?

In the United States, ramen may still be best known as a college-dorm standby, those ten-for-a-dollar pouches of fried noodles and seasoning packets, but that's changing as enthusiasm and demand for craft ramen surges. In New York City, where I live, that cultural shift happened when David Chang opened his restaurant Momofuku in 2004. Vegetarian ramen, however, has been slower to the scene. Momofuku famously didn't even offer one until ten years later, in 2014. Other ramen shops that added a vegetarian option to their menus seemed to do so only as an afterthought—usually a watery or over-salty bowl of miso soup with some noodles and tofu tossed in. But Chuko's vegetarian ramen inspired me. It was an exercise in balance, with a structured, flavorful broth at the heart; fresh, tender, slithery wheat noodles as the backbone; and a changing cast of seasonal vegetables as texture and flavor adornments.

I set out to work on my own recipe. As I suspected, the secret was a good broth. But unlike recipes for traditional ramen broth—which require hours, if not days, of roasting and simmering, and much money spent on meat and bones—a delicious vegetarian adaptation is not difficult, time-consuming, or expensive. Instead, it involves the easiest soup stock I've ever made: dashi, a kelp-based broth that's central to Japanese cuisine.

The basic formula—savory broth, noodles, and assorted condiments—is much the same for the Vietnamese dish pho. Pho boasts a more vegetable-oriented and fragrant broth, with heady warm spices, rice noodles swapped for the wheat ones, and handfuls of fresh herbs. The combination of nutritious broth, noodles, and abundant seasonal vegetables becomes a well-rounded meal.

Korea's bibimbap is equally easy to adapt to a vegetarian dish. It contains rice instead of broth and noodles, and arrives sizzling at the table in a hot stoneware serving vessel (called a *dolsot*), topped with fresh and pickled vegetables, protein of some sort, and a fried or sometimes raw egg that's cracked into the hot rice and vigorously stirred in. A few squirts of chili sauce meld everything together.

Other grains—quinoa, bulgur, polenta, and even oatmeal—form the basis of bowls that are contemporary cousins of bibimbap. The rule is the same as with bibimbap: Put everything you need for a well-rounded meal into a single serving vessel. In goes the grain; a few different vegetables, some cooked, some marinated or lightly dressed, some raw; maybe a poached or soft-boiled egg or a few cubes of tofu; and then a dollop of a flavorful condiment.

With the bowl as organizing principle, vegetarian Chinese- or Japanese-style dumplings—whether steamed, boiled, or fried—can be served in soups, over salads, or over a combination of kale and quinoa. You can fill the dumplings with bean sprouts, scallions, and sometimes tofu, with flavorings of soy, ginger, garlic, and chives. Exercising more creative license, I found that fillings of summer squash, carrots, and parsnips, or kale and chickpeas are equally delicious.

Once you get a handle on the balance of these elements, you're free to experiment. Work with your own preferences, or whatever produce you have on hand. *Bowl* is packed with the kinds of simple techniques that help a cook gain confidence: salting summer squash to prevent it from becoming mushy; roasting shiitake mushrooms for a savory, juicy component of a rice bowl; shallow-frying rings of shallot or wisps of scallion for an irresistible, salty, crunchy topping for pretty much anything; flame-roasting a small eggplant or jalapeño pepper; toasting quinoa, which results in excellent batches every time; sprouting lentils for a nutrient powerhouse bowl base or condiment; blistering cherry tomatoes or searing scallions in a skillet; sprinkling a fried egg with soy sauce in the last minute or so to give some umami to its flavor profile—and much more.

I love the light, clean fullness of these bowls, and I especially love their built-in seasonal variety. I eat them all year long. Summer Ramen (page 50), for instance—what a dish! If a piping hot bowl of ramen doesn't sound like what you want to eat on a balmy August day, I do understand—but still, you must try it. Its flavors—a corn-based dashi broth, summery ripe tomatoes, and lots of basil as garnish—are so pure, its unity of components so straightforward and harmonious, its overall effect so quintessentially summery, that it's a reward and a redemption at the same time.

tools and ingredients

Making the bowls in this book doesn't require anything too specialized or expensive, but there are a number of tools and ingredients that may not already be in your kitchen, but are worth seeking out. In this chapter, I'll guide you through outfitting your kitchen and pantry to most efficiently cook and serve the dishes in this book. For a few items, you'll want to visit a restaurant supply store, Asian market, or online retailer (see Sources, page 249).

tools

STOCKPOTS AND SAUCEPANS

If you are buying stockpots and saucepans, think long-term. Buy heavy, sturdy ones, which are much more versatile and long lasting than lightweight versions and distribute heat more evenly. Avoid nonstick options because the coating can scratch off easily, leaving gray bits floating in the soup.

Large stockpot: Making vegetable stock or pho broth in a pot that's too small is a miserable challenge. Choose one that's at least 8 quarts and ideally 12, with a heavy bottom.

3-quart saucepan: Ideal for cooking rice and grains, blanching vegetables, and for heating up all the different kinds of broth in this book. I find a wide saucepan, sometimes called a *saucier,* which has a wider base and opening than a saucepan, to be more versatile than one with a smaller base and straighter sides.

Small, 1-quart saucepan: Great for smaller needs, such as poaching eggs, cooking small batches of rice or other grains, heating up enough broth for one or two servings, and the like.

STRAINING TOOLS

Pasta insert: You'll need a stockpot with a pasta insert to rinse Asian noodles to remove starch, which makes them slicker and more slurpable, while also reserving the water so they can be easily rewarmed. These sets are sometimes sold as multicookers or pasta pots.

Strainer basket: Even handier than a pasta insert is a long-handled basket made from wires or mesh, which can hold single servings of noodles or dumplings as they cook. Lift the noodles out of the boiling water, thoroughly rinse them off, quickly dunk them back in the water to rewarm them, then transfer them to the individual bowls. The second best option is to use a fine-mesh sieve.

Large (8-inch) fine-mesh sieve: This is one of my favorite tools in the kitchen for straining stock; boiling rice, dumplings, and blanched greens; blanching mung bean sprouts; rinsing rice or quinoa; and so much more. Choose a fine-mesh sieve made from heavy-duty—rather than lightweight and malleable—mesh, with a sturdy, metal frame and handle.

Spider skimmer: A version of a slotted spoon, this important tool is wider in diameter, with the metal wire spoon part affixed to a long handle that is usually made of lightweight bamboo. It's designed for removing items like boiled dumplings and stray greens from big pots. It's also good for getting eggs into and out of the water when boiling them.

Colander: A large colander can act as a frame for a few layers of cheesecloth when straining large quantities of vegetable stock. Its holes are typically too large for grains, which pass right through.

Cheesecloth: Making stock and pho broth is time-consuming, and you should maximize your profits. So when straining the broth, line your sieve or colander with a few layers of cheesecloth first. Pour or ladle the liquid through the lined colander. Then once the stock has cooled to a safe temperature, collect the corners of the cheesecloth, gathering up all of the solids, and gently squeeze, so as to extract as much precious liquid as possible.

SKILLETS

A **good-sized skillet** is necessary for pan-frying vegetables and making crispy-bottomed rice for bibimbap. When feeding a crowd, a **large 12- or even 15-inch skillet** allows cooking all at once rather than in batches, but otherwise a **10-inch**

skillet does the job well. For basic, all-purpose use, I've tried out lots of different materials—cast-iron, stainless steel, enamel cast-iron, and nonstick—and I prefer stainless steel. Oven-safe skillets—those with metal, not plastic, handles—are the most versatile. Cast-iron skillets are a wonderful inexpensive option but require extra care so they don't rust. A **small, 6-inch, cast-iron skillet** is useful for smaller jobs—like frying up an egg or toasting a handful of whole spices.

A **medium-sized nonstick skillet** comes in handy in these recipes for things like sautéing delicate slabs of tofu and is wonderful for fried rice—so much easier to clean than anything else. Be sure to wash nonstick skillets gently, so that you don't scrape through the coating.

STACKING STEAMER UNIT

You'll need a stacking bamboo steamer unit like the ones you see at dim sum restaurants, in which the layers fit into one another and are capped with a lid.

The genius of a stacking unit is that you can steam several different layers at a time. To use it, fill a skillet with a half-inch or so of water, set the steamer unit in the skillet, bring the water to a simmer, then fill the layers with the foods to be steamed. The steam rises from the bottom, cooking everything at once. This is great for steaming dumplings in any quantity as well as for cooking multiple vegetables simultaneously. Just use caution when opening up the lid—steam burns.

MANDOLINE OR JAPANESE MANDOLINE

A French tool used for slicing, shaving, shredding, and julienning foods into uniform slivers, slabs, or strips, a mandoline makes the job easier and the results more uniform. French mandolines can be quite expensive and intimidating looking, but cheaper Japanese models, made mostly from plastic, are a great alternative.

Use caution when working with a mandoline. Work slowly and carefully, and don't look up from it, or you risk slicing your finger on the blade. Most Japanese mandolines come with a plastic, pronged device that functions as something of a handle for your food—it fits between the food and your hand—and it works fine until you get to the last stub of vegetable. You can also buy mesh metal gloves or gloves made from cut-resistant material, which make the process significantly safer.

RICE COOKER

There's a reason that those who cook a lot of rice—in particular, most Asian households—have a rice cooker in the kitchen. Not only does it eliminate a lot of the margin for error associated with stovetop rice-cooking methods, but it also eliminates a pan, which is especially useful for the component-style of cooking featured in this book. Most models have a function that keeps cooked rice warm for up to several hours, which further makes for one less thing to worry about when you're scrambling to get a hot meal to the table.

Look for rice cookers that have settings for both white and brown rice. For the recipes in this book, a medium-sized rice cooker, which has a capacity of 5 to 6 cups cooked rice, is ideal. If your rice cooker is made by a Japanese manufacturer, just be aware that the cup that comes with a Japanese rice cooker is typically 180 ml, whereas an American cup is 240 ml. Use the cup that comes with your machine to measure both the rice and water, according to the manufacturer's instructions.

One US cup of dry rice will yield about 2½ cups cooked rice, but the 180 ml cup from the Japanese machine will yield slightly less than 2 cups cooked. If your rice cooker has a nonstick lining, which does make for easy cleaning, be sure to use a plastic or wooden spatula for scooping out the cooked rice, to avoid scratching it.

MORTAR AND PESTLE

You'll use this to crush whole spices, grind sesame seeds into coarse powder, turn fresh ginger into a zingy condiment, and more. An electric spice mill, a mini food processor, or even a knife and cutting board can replicate the effect in most cases, but the mortar and pestle can coax more flavors and natural oils out of the food and give you more control over the texture.

Simply place whatever needs grinding into the mortar, then use the pestle to tap-tap-tap it into submission. Occasionally, such as when grinding a whole spice into a fine powder, you'll need to use a circular, grinding motion and a bit more muscle. But the heavy weight and coarse texture of a mortar and pestle mean that gravity and friction do most of the work.

A tall, deep one is ideal, with a capacity of 2 to 3 cups. Smaller mortars can get messy when grinding up any more than a tablespoon or so of spices or seeds.

IMMERSION BLENDER

One important step in preparing the ramen broths in this book is to thoroughly puree miso paste with a ladleful of dashi and other flavorings before adding them back to the pot of broth. This can be done in a standard blender, but it's much simpler with an immersion bender, which is basically a wand with rotating blades that puree the liquid right in the container. Most come with a tall plastic cup, which is the perfect vessel to use for this blitzing step.

SERVING WARE

You're definitely going to need bowls! Unfortunately, the Western-sized soup bowl is too small for these recipes. You can always serve smaller portions, but properly sized ramen bowls are inexpensive and easy to find and have the perk of doubling as medium-sized mixing bowls when you're running short in other cooking projects. Ramen bowls can usually hold about 1 quart and are made from ceramic, earthenware, or another material that allows them to be relatively heat-safe.

Chopsticks are not essential for ramen, pho, and bibimbap, but they are traditional, and, in my opinion, improve the dining experience. Brothy dishes are traditionally slurped up with dumpling spoons or by lifting the ramen bowl to your lips and sipping directly from it.

Most Japanese markets and many restaurant supply stores sell all of these things. Well-stocked houseware stores like Crate & Barrel and Pottery Barn that have a good selection of inexpensive, basic white pieces usually carry ramen bowls, and these same stores usually have a few different options for chopsticks and dumpling spoons as well.

ingredients

I choose to support health and sustainability through my produce-buying power. In general I prefer produce that has travelled the shortest distance from point of origin to point of sale, and prefer shopping at a farmers' market so I can support my local economy. Growers are usually on hand to answer questions about seasonality, organics, and other growing practices. Community Supported Agriculture (CSA) programs, roadside farm stands, and mindfully curated grocery stores are all good places to shop for produce if you share these concerns.

Ginger: I love how ginger changes so dramatically as it cooks, from a fresh flowery heat when grated raw to a deep, warm-spice layer of flavor (think gingerbread) when exposed to prolonged heat. In pho broth, the whole piece of ginger is blackened over a flame or under a broiler to draw out even more of its nuances. Always buy ginger that's firm all over. I prefer the smaller, less mature roots—in which the thickest parts are about the thickness of a forefinger—as these tend to be juicier and have a brighter flavor. Make sure to seek out organic ginger, or source it from your local farmers' market.

To peel ginger, some cooks like to use a spoon, but when I do that I lose too much flesh. Instead, I use the back of a knife. A paring knife works well, but so does a chef's knife. Young, thin-skinned ginger requires just a gentle scrape up and down; more mature ginger requires a bit more force. It takes a few tries to get the hang of this, but once you do, it's very easy and efficient.

Scallions: I use both the white and green parts. Most often I trim them of the roots and any frayed or discolored pieces on the other end, and then slice them thinly and sprinkle over a dish before serving. Scallions treated this way are more than a garnish; they are sharp and slightly sweet and a powerful foil to saltiness and richness.

Scallions purchased from the farmers' market will be more flavorful than the ones found at the grocery store, but they will need to be washed more thoroughly. Stored roots-down in a tall glass filled with about an inch of water, they'll keep for weeks, and will even begin to replenish themselves.

Hearty greens: Kale, spinach, and Swiss chard are used the most in this book, but feel free to substitute beet and turnip greens, mustard and dandelion greens, mature arugula, collards, leaf amaranth, or any other greens you come across. In most cases they should be cooked just until wilted, either by boiling, steaming, or sautéing.

Most recipes in this book instruct you to remove the tough, fibrous stems of greens like kale, because their crunchy texture is distracting in the finished dish. But if you're in the habit of eating the stems, disregard the stemming steps. My favorite technique is to roll up the greens and chiffonade them—cut them into the thinnest possible ribbons—which makes the stems so small that they're hardly noticeable.

Herbs: Particularly in delicate vegetarian dishes, herbs are essential for fresh, forthright flavor. In pho this is especially true, since the pile of fresh herbs served alongside the soup is one of its defining characteristics.

Wash herbs right when you bring them home, then dry them thoroughly and store in airtight bags or containers in the fridge. This applies to basil, cilantro, parsley, chives, mint, and all other herbs in general. This way they'll keep for up to a week, sometimes more, and will be ready for you right when you want them.

Watercress: Spicy and bitter wild greens such as watercress and arugula are extremely healthful, in part because they haven't been cultivated to taste sweet (a process that has depleted lots of other vegetables of many of their healthful properties).

In these recipes, watercress is used as much for flavor and texture as for its visual effects as a garnish. Look for bunches that contain few or no wilted leaves or wet splotches of dark green leaves, which indicate the early stages of spoilage. Stems should be crisp, not rubbery, with very little browning at the cut. When you get home, remove the rubber band from around the stems—this is always where watercress starts to go bad—and wash thoroughly. Once dry and stored in an airtight bag or container in the fridge, it'll keep for a week or more. Farmers' markets will have the best, spiciest watercress, but it's widely available at supermarkets.

Sprouts and shoots: Bean and seed sprouts and shoots are simply the beginning stage of seeds turning into plants. Shoots are the more mature of the two, with longer stems and a leaf or two; they have been clipped to remove the seed or bean. Sprouts and shoots are a wonderful source of concentrated nutrients, and in these recipes, they function as an easy way to add fresh flavors, texture, health benefits, and a pretty garnish to the bowls. Most grocery stores, particularly health food stores, have a few different varieties of shoots and sprouts to choose from, including broccoli, radish, sunflower, mung bean, and alfalfa. These can all be used, though for the recipes in this book the ones with the crunchiest texture work best. The farmers' market is the best place to buy shoots, particularly in the spring. And it's not difficult to grow sprouts at home—for instructions, see the Sprouted Lentil Bowl recipe on page 158.

Fresh sprouts are quite perishable and should be stored in the refrigerator and used within a day or two of purchasing or sprouting. It's also important to wash them well before using. Heartier ones like mung bean sprouts need to be blanched in boiling water before use, as instructed in the recipes, to soften their raw texture and flavor.

NOODLES

Finding good, fresh ramen noodles—even in cities that are hubs for international cuisines—can be a real challenge. Grocery stores tend to carry only one or two brands of dried Chinese wheat noodles or *chuka soba*. These are better than the ones found in instant ramen pouches, but they're not exactly noteworthy. Visiting a Japanese market or Asian grocery store will give you many more dried noodle options and sometimes a few good fresh ones.

Ramen: I go into more detail about the particular of ramen noodles and include a recipe for them on page 232, but very generally speaking, noodles meant for ramen are firm but buoyant and bright yellow in color. Packages of fresh noodles should contain just wheat, water, sometimes salt, and finally, alkali, which is really the distinguishing factor. Chinese versions of these noodles tend to also contain egg. For dried noodles, look for Chinese wheat noodles, Japanese *chuka soba*, or lo mein. I also occasionally substitute rice noodles for wheat in my ramen—I love the Forbidden Rice Ramen noodles made by Lotus Foods—especially if I'm serving a friend with a gluten sensitivity. Or you can also substitute soba, udon, or even Italian-style spaghetti or linguini, depending on what you have on hand.

If you find a brand of fresh or dried ramen noodles that you like, by all means, stock up (fresh noodles can be stored in the freezer). Sun Noodle is a leading manufacturer of fresh ramen noodles for restaurants across the country and is considered one of the best US-based makers. They also have a small retail program and a store locator on their website (see Sources, page 250).

Rice noodles: Used in pho and some cold vermicelli salads, these are typically made from just rice flour and water, or sometimes include a bit of starch to improve the texture. For the recipes in this book, look for medium-width—slightly less than ¼ inch, roughly the same size as Italian fettuccini—in boxes or bags. At grocery stores, these are sometimes marked "Pad Thai" noodles. Asian grocery stores carry a much better selection and offer larger package sizes (usually 1-pound packages instead of 8-ounce). Check the bag or box to make sure the noodles haven't been broken. My favorite brand is Royal Elephant, available at specialty stores and online. Brown rice noodles can be used in the same way, though I haven't been pleased with every brand I've tried—many are gummy when reconstituted. The brown rice vermicelli made by King Soba, though, is very good.

In bowls of ramen and pho, the volume of broth needs to match the quantity of noodles so that you're not left with a pile of noodles after you finish the broth or vice versa. My preference is a ratio of 3 to 4 ounces of cooked noodles (1½ to 2 ounces dried) to 1½ cups broth per bowl. For fresh noodles, 12 to 16 ounces is sufficient to serve four.

SOBA

FRESH RAMEN

UDON

Soba: There are several easy-to-find brands of organic soba, a style of Japanese buckwheat noodles, available at well-stocked grocery stores. Most brands have a 100 percent buckwheat option as well as others that are cut with wheat or yam flour to soften the texture and add some elasticity. (One hundred percent buckwheat is grittier than what most of us are used to when it comes to noodles.) I prefer slightly thicker soba noodles to the thinner ones, and my favorites are made by Sobaya. They're not 100 percent buckwheat, but they're a bit longer than most other soba noodle brands, and are sold in 1-pound boxes rather than the usual 11.5-ounce bags. I love their tender structure and clean flavor.

DUMPLING WRAPPERS

Asian dumpling wrappers, or skins, come in a few different varieties. Most grocery stores carry square and round wrappers, sometimes labeled "wonton" and "gyoza," respectively, and different brands come in different thicknesses. White wrappers should typically only contain flour and water; yellow ones often contain egg.

Square or round and white or yellow varieties can be used for the recipes in this book. For most vegetarian dumplings, thin wrappers are preferable, because thicker wrappers compete with the flavors of the filling. The exception is fried dumplings or potstickers, in which case you want thicker, white, round dumpling wrappers. Thin versions don't hold up as well when fried—they turn into just a brittle crust— whereas the thicker wrappers retain some chewiness.

When buying dumpling wrappers, poke and gently bend the package to make sure that they are fresh and pliant. Also make sure they're not dried out around the edges—this is usually visible as a white, brittle border—and that no moisture has been trapped inside, which makes the wrappers congeal. At the grocery store, look in both the refrigerated and the frozen sections. Twin Marquis is a readily available and consistently good brand. Asian markets have a much better selection of dumpling wrappers and a higher turnover than Western grocery stores do.

Once purchased, dumpling wrappers need to be frozen or refrigerated. Most often the ones you find at the grocery store have been frozen, and it's usually fine to refreeze them. Use them within a few days if you keep them in the refrigerator, and within a month or two if you keep them in the freezer. The longer they sit around, the more they dry out. If your dumpling wrappers start to develop dry edges, trim them off with a sharp knife and reduce the filling amount accordingly.

I used to gravitate toward white rice—in traditional Asian cuisines white rice is preferred to brown—but once I figured out a better cooking method for brown rice (see page 222), I came to prefer its more complex flavor and texture. The only challenge is that it takes more than twice as long as white rice to cook. Setting it to soak in the morning is one way to cut back on the cooking time.

Long-grain rice: Long-grain rice is best for bibimbaps, and jasmine is one of my favorites. It has a lightly floral flavor and typically cooks into a gorgeous, fluffy indulgence. It's available in both white and brown varieties, and the brown is very good, though it cooks up a little less fluffy than the white. Domestic long-grain white and brown rice can also be used.

Medium-grain rice: Chewier medium-grain rice is my preference for some of the bowls in the Grain chapter. I love heritage rice and brown sushi rice in these types of applications as well.

Rice should always be rinsed. White rice in particular has a lot of extra starch clinging to its exterior, and thoroughly rinsing it will keep it from turning into a sticky mess. This applies both to rice cooked on the stovetop and rice cooked in a rice cooker.

If you're concerned about buying and cooking organic produce, that concern should extend to your rice and grains, which, after all, are also plants. I'm a fan of the widely distributed Lundberg brand, which has many organic options for domestic and imported rice. Lotus Foods's options for rice are also very good, though a little harder to find. The bulk section of grocery stores that have high turnover is a great place to shop.

WILD RICE

POLENTA

FARRO

SHORT-GRAIN
(SUSHI) RICE

BLACK
(FORBIDDEN)
RICE

QUINOA

Farro: Farro is a terrifically chewy grain with a bold wheat flavor, and a good one to work into your regular repertoire. You can speed up its cooking time by soaking the grains for a few hours before cooking. For the most attractive results, cover the farro with cold water and then bring the pot to boil, as opposed to adding the grains to already boiling water. This way the husks don't split.

Polenta: A pot of gurgling polenta is a comforting sight when it's cold out, and the polenta bowl that appears on page 130 is one of my favorite dishes in this book. The coarseness of the grind will determine the cooking time. I recommend seeking out coarse-ground polenta—the cooking time is longer, but the finished dish will have a more luxurious texture.

Quinoa: Quinoa is available in a range of colors—white, black, and red, which can all be used interchangeably. Some quinoa is sold "pre-rinsed," meaning that it's been rinsed of its bitter outer casing called saponin. If your package is not labeled as such, make sure to thoroughly wash it in a fine-mesh sieve under cold running water before proceeding. And as with some of the other grains, toasting it first in a bit of oil improves its flavor.

SEA VEGETABLES

Sea vegetables have long been a staple of Japanese cuisine in raw, dried, and fermented forms. They are hugely nutritious—particularly as a source of calcium, but also for dozens of other vitamins and minerals—and are a source of rich umami flavor, as they contain naturally occurring glutamates, one of the elements of synthetically produced MSG. I use a few of the most commonly available sea vegetables in this book.

Kombu: The basis of the stocks and broths in this book, kombu is perhaps the most important of the sea vegetables in Japanese cuisine. There are many varieties from wide and flat ones to long and narrow ones, and they all taste different. As a general rule, the more expensive the kombu, the better its quality. Most common at supermarkets are flat rectangles or squares, which are usually available in one or two different brands. Japanese markets have a much vaster selection, often sold in much larger, more rustic-looking pieces. When I get home, I trim big pieces into 2-inch squares, each of which is sufficient for one serving. Some cooks recommend wiping the residual white powder off the kombu, but I don't, since the white powder contains flavor and minerals. Emerald Cove sells kombu from the Pacific Ocean, harvested off the Northern China coast. From the Atlantic Ocean, Maine Coast Sea Vegetables is an easy-to-find label.

Nori: Sometimes labeled as "laver," particularly in English-speaking countries outside the United States, nori is most recognizable as the blackish-green wrap used for sushi rolls and hand rolls. Harvested algae is ground up, flattened into sheets, and dried in a way similar to how paper is produced. If you're looking to cut back on salt, crumbled nori is a great alternative.

Most nori available at the grocery store is already toasted, but before using it, it's best to quickly heat it to bring out its flavor: Just wave it over a gas flame turned to high until it curls slightly and gets crisp. If you don't have a gas range, you can also roast it under a broiler, watching the whole time and flipping it periodically. Immediately slice the sheet into very thin wisps with a chef's knife, or use your fingers to crumble it over your dish.

Maine Coast Sea Vegetables makes a very good certified organic line of nori that's imported from China, as well as an Atlantic-harvested line of laver, which can be used in the same way. It's raw and should be cooked first over low heat to crisp it for crumbling (check the instructions on the back of the package). Emerald Cove and Eden Foods sell premium lines of nori, imported from Japan. Both companies are well distributed and their products are available through online retailers. Make sure you don't buy seasoned nori, which is intended as a snack.

Wakame: An antioxidant-rich, frilly-looking sea vegetable sold either in minced pieces or in whole leaves, dried wakame should be chopped after reconstituting. It has a silky texture and sweet flavor, and I find it to be hugely versatile in salads and soups. I always buy the bigger pieces, rather than the preshredded, and chop it myself. Maine Coast Sea Vegetables harvests alaria, which is wakame's Atlantic coast counterpart, and Emerald Cove and Eden Foods offer wakame imported from Japan.

Soy sauce is a product that has been made for over three thousand years from fermented soybeans and wheat, brine, and yeast. Most cuisines of Asia have a take on soy sauce to call their own. I highly recommend tasting a few brands to see what you like best. Soy sauce is a food product with a great deal of history, variety, and complexity, and can hold up to the same scrutinizing curiosity that food lovers apply to other elemental foods like honey, vinegar, and olive oil.

Koikuchi shoyu: In these recipes I primarily use easy-to-find "dark" Japanese-style soy sauce, known in Japan as *koikuchi shoyu*. I opt for those made from organic soybeans, and two relatively easy-to-find brands are San-J and Eden Organic. Mitoku also has a very good line of traditional soy sauce, which is my favorite but can be difficult to find, and Kikkoman has an organic label of soy sauce. (Most soy sauce available at US markets is *koikuchi shoyu*, so unless it is marked otherwise, this is a safe assumption.) I'm not a fan of low-salt soy sauce, as it tastes watery by comparison.

Tamari: If you have a gluten sensitivity, opt for tamari, another Japanese soy sauce that's usually made entirely from soy, rather than soy and wheat. Make sure to choose one that's marked gluten-free, as some varieties contain small amounts of gluten. Mitoku, San-J, and Eden Organic all make organic and gluten-free tamari.

Kecap manis: Indonesian soy sauce, or *kecap manis*, is one of my favorite condiments. It's a thick, sweet soy sauce with hints of warm spices and deep molasses notes. I love it drizzled over steamed dumplings, or over a plain bowl of rice. It's also great in dressings and marinades. ABC brand is my favorite and the easiest to find. Look for it at specialty stores, Asian markets, and online retailers.

MISO

Miso is a fermented paste typically made from soybeans, grain, salt, and *kojikin*, a culture similar to what's used to transform milk into cheese. Like soy sauce, its culinary tradition dates back thousands of years, and it's a central ingredient in Japanese cuisine. Miso is a protein- and nutrient-rich ingredient, and the basis of the fortifying soup of the same name.

Good miso has a rich, rounded umami flavor profile, and it's delicious enough that you can eat it right off a spoon. There are hundreds of different types, but you can usually only find red, black, and white misos outside of Japanese markets. The darker the color, the more assertive the flavor of the miso tends to be; by contrast, lighter-colored misos have a milder, sweeter flavor. In this book I use light-colored miso. But if you purchase a dark miso and a light one, you can combine the two to create a more complex flavor base.

Most miso pastes are gluten-free and vegetarian. Be sure to check the label, as some have trace amounts of wheat and I've come across some brands that list dried fish products among the ingredients. As with most soy products, I prefer organic miso pastes, and the best ones I've tasted are by South River Miso, which makes traditional, coarse-textured miso pastes, as well as varieties made from chickpeas and adzuki beans. Miso Master is another US-based company that makes traditional-style miso pastes that are widely available at supermarkets and health food stores.

SALT

In this book's recipes, fine sea salt should be used unless otherwise noted. Most refined, inexpensive table salt or kosher salt is processed, and the manufacturing procedure strips away everything but the sodium itself—in particular the minerals, imparted by the ocean water or the land at the location of the harvest or the salt mine. Additives are later thrown back in, usually to preserve the color and prevent caking. In culinary terms, this means that what you taste is only salt and often a slight sourness and bitterness. Minimally processed sea salts, by contrast, retain almost all of the dozens of trace minerals that are present at the time of harvest. Not only does this offer some health perks, but it also affects the finished dish with a fuller savory profile—the flavor of the ocean. Additionally, sea salt doesn't taste as "salty" as table salt or kosher salt.

Taste a few different types of salt, unadorned, and see what differences you notice, then play around with them in your cooking. Keep in mind that the size of the crystal will affect measurements—a teaspoon of fine sea salt is heavier by weight, as it is more tightly packed in the spoon than a teaspoon of bulkier, coarse-textured salt, so adjust the amounts appropriately.

OIL AND VINEGAR

Neutral-tasting oil: Olive oil is what most people I know cook with, but it has a lower smoke point and an assertive flavor that doesn't meld well with Asian flavor profiles. Light-flavored olive oil can sometimes be used, but make sure to not let it burn. For the recipes in *Bowl,* I cook primarily with organic, non-GMO canola oil. Rice bran oil is another (more costly) option. Skip vegetable oil and any oils that contain corn or soybean oil. Spectrum is a good, widely available brand with many organic options, all of which are non-GMO.

Toasted sesame oil: Toasted sesame oil, sometimes labeled "roasted," is different from pale-colored sesame oil. It's made from toasted or roasted sesame seeds, which make it toffee-colored and gives it a very assertive, highly aromatic flavor. Untoasted sesame oil has a much higher smoke point and can be used for cooking, but toasted sesame oil should be thought of as a finishing oil and shouldn't be exposed to high heat. It's typically available in small, 4- to 8-ounce bottles. Spectrum and Eden Foods both have lines of toasted sesame oil that are non-GMO, and the former has an organic option. The most dependably available brand is Kadoya.

Rice vinegar and brown rice vinegar: The primary acids of choice in this book, rice vinegars are used for quick-pickling, for seasoning rice, and in sauces, dressings, and marinades. Brown and white rice vinegars are both relatively mellow and can be used interchangeably in my recipes. The brown variety has a slightly better nutritional profile and fuller flavor, so I prefer it. You'll often see "seasoned" rice vinegar on the same shelf at the grocery store. This just means that salt and sugar (and sometimes a few other things) have been added—many cooks use this pre-seasoned vinegar to flavor sushi rice. I prefer the unseasoned varieties, since it seems a lot more straightforward to just add salt and sugar myself, and that's what you should use for the recipes in *Bowl*. My favorite organic brown rice vinegar is made by Mitoku. Marukan is another good organic brand, and it's made domestically.

DRIED SHIITAKE MUSHROOMS

Dried shiitake mushrooms add a great deal of depth to vegetarian stocks and soups—some call it a "meaty" flavor—and I use them liberally in these recipes. They're common in Japanese and Chinese cuisines, significantly more so than in Western ones, so the best place to buy them is at Asian markets, where the turnover is more frequent. There, you can get a large bag or buy them in bulk for a better price than the small pouches carried at supermarkets and health food stores.

Choose mushrooms that look good—like mushrooms rather than calcified mushroom remains—and are still somewhat pliable. If it's possible to smell them prior to purchase, give them a whiff: They should be heady with a deep, earthy, complex scent. You'll only use the caps for eating, but those that still have some of the stem attached are generally considered of better quality than those without. Store them in an airtight container or resealable bag at room temperature in your pantry.

SESAME SEEDS

Sesame seeds pack a great nutritional punch—they're full of nutrients and have a good amount of protein given their size—and should be thought of as an ingredient worthy of showcasing.

Unhulled sesame seeds are less processed than hulled, which, as with whole grains, makes them a bit more nutrient dense (in particular, they contain significantly more calcium than the hulled variety). Hulled and unhulled can be used interchangeably in these recipes, and the same goes for black and white sesame seeds. In all cases look for raw sesame seeds and store them in an airtight jar or bag in the refrigerator, as they're quite perishable. Before cooking, toast them briefly in a dry skillet over low heat until fragrant, which intensifies their flavor.

Buy them in the bulk aisle of grocery and health food stores that see a lot of turnover. Bob's Red Mill, Shiloh Farms, and Arrowhead Mills also sell sesame seeds by the bag, available through online retailers and at well-stocked stores.

CONDIMENTS

Gochujang: A fermented chili paste and a staple of the Korean pantry, *gochujang* is used like Westerners use tomato paste. It's a thick, spicy, savory, slightly funky-tasting blend of dried chilies, fermented soybeans, rice, and salt. Some brands contain trace amounts of wheat, so check the label if you have a gluten sensitivity. *Gochujang* is used in this book to make the condiment for bibimbap (Gochujang Sauce, page 242), and in a few other places as a seasoning agent. *Gochujang* is worth seeking out, especially if you like sriracha. It's terrific stirred into some mayonnaise and used as a dip or sandwich condiment, or added to the filling for deviled eggs, and certainly in all kinds of marinades and dressings.

Mother-in-Law's Kimchi, a small, US-based company, recently released its own *gochujang*. Asian and specifically Korean markets carry several different options, available in glass jars and rectangular plastic tubs. It's also easy to find online. Look for brands that don't list high-fructose corn syrup or MSG in the ingredients, and note that the paste itself is different from the squeeze bottles marked *"gochujang* sauce."

Sambal oelek: The store-bought version of this vibrant Indonesian condiment is a fixture of the Asian aisle of the grocery store. I cook with it all the time, in dishes other than those of Indonesian origin. Anytime you see "chili-garlic paste" in this book, you can use *sambal oelek,* or try my recipe for a homemade *sambal* (page 241).

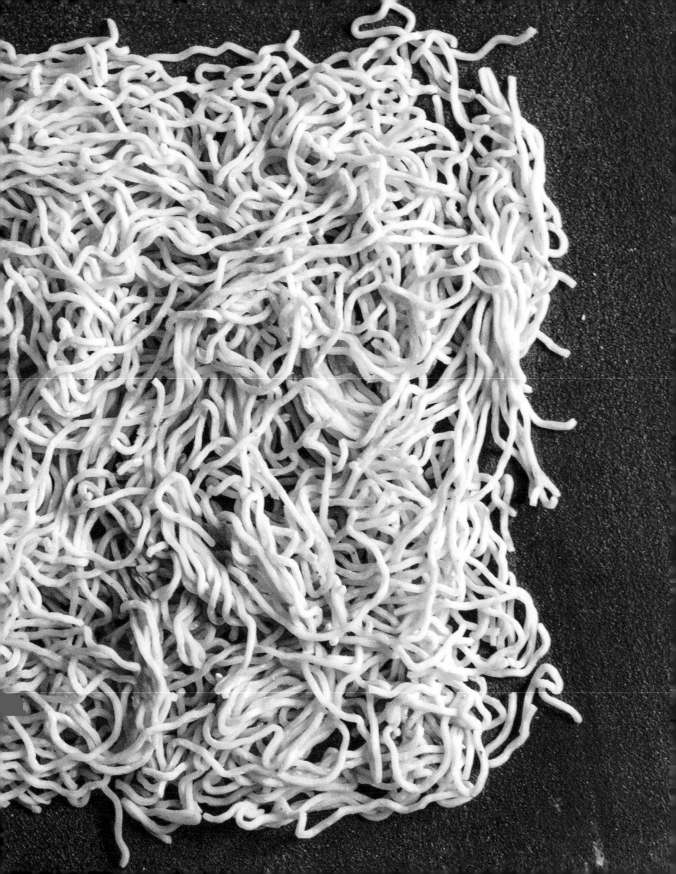

ramen and other wheat noodle bowls

Ramen is a simple dish of rich, savory broth, tender noodles, and some assortment of protein, vegetables, and condiments. With the emanating heat, rich and inviting aromas, colorful toppings, variety of flavors and textures, and the *thhhhhhhssssssssck* of slurping noodles, it's a real experience for the senses.

Ramen allegedly originated in China, where it was made from hand-pulled wheat noodles. During the second half of the nineteenth century, as a result of Japan's expansion into China, ramen found its way to Japan, and has since been primarily associated with the Japanese. Like many great dishes, ramen is the result of cultures intermingling. It has undergone much modification and evolution over the decades—it may be a different thing entirely from what was originally tasted in China, which some argue makes it a Japanese rather than Chinese dish in origin. Flash-forward a hundred or so years to the United States' post–World War II occupation of Japan in the latter half of the twentieth century, where Americans encountered ramen, allowing its delicious reputation to spread on more of a global scale.

And perhaps even more significantly, in 1958 Nissin Foods developed a method for deep-frying wheat noodles and shaping them into rectangles or cones. This created a quick way to later cook the noodles, which is how instant ramen and Cup Noodles came to be. Instant ramen took off in Japan, found its way around the globe beginning in the 1970s, and has been a staple of grocery stores and college dorm rooms ever since. The popularity of both the instant style and the much celebrated "ramen-shop" style of noodles have turned this dish into a subject of much speculation, excitement, and debate. There are museums, documentaries, cookbooks, and academic texts devoted to ramen. My overview is very brief.

It's worth mentioning that longstanding traditions for vegetarian ramen are slim if not nonexistent. I've tried lots of vegetarian ramen at restaurants in many different cities and all of them are different—from a cloudy ginger-miso broth enriched with soy milk to a barely opaque ramen broth that tastes purely, and pleasantly, of dried chilies. Every bowl seems to showcase a different type of noodle. By and large, most are made from vegetarian dashi and flavored with miso.

This chapter focuses on wheat noodle bowls, primarily ramen. Beyond that, I've provided vegetarian adaptations for other traditional dishes: the refreshing Japanese Zaru Soba, spicy Malaysian Curry Laksa, and the Indonesian boiled vegetable salad Gado-Gado, which is sometimes served over Chinese wheat noodles. Then there are some unorthodox favorites, perfect for packing up to take on picnics and road trips, like the cold Cashew-Scallion Noodles and Black Sesame Noodle Bowl.

salting the cooking water and rinsing the noodles

When cooking Italian pasta, the custom is to generously salt the cooking water so that it tastes "like the sea," with the result that the noodles are seasoned all the way through and that the toppings and sauce need not be aggressively seasoned.

In Asian preparations, however, this is not the case. Noodles, whether rice or wheat, are traditionally cooked in plain boiling water. The reasoning varies a bit, but I've gleaned that it's because so many of the toppings are rich in salt and other fermented and umami flavors like soy and miso. Additionally, some packaged dry noodles contain more salt than their Italian counterparts (though this is not true across the board—many recipes of Chinese and Japanese wheat noodles contain no salt at all).

Still, I find that some noodles, like soba noodles, and some dishes, like ramen and cold noodle preparations, benefit from salting the cooking water because it provides a better balance of seasoning in the finished dish. If I don't salt the cooking water, I sometimes have to make up for it with extra soy sauce or salt, and the results feel skewed. I take it on a case-by-case basis. Feel free to play around as you cook these recipes, but I've marked those where I find salting the cooking water to be beneficial.

Additionally, the "slurp" factor—the slippery, slithery quality—is an important one with most Asian noodle dishes, and this is especially so for ramen and pho. To achieve it, cooked noodles are always rinsed under cold water, which removes all the surface starch and makes them more slick—ideal for slurping. Using a strainer basket or the strainer insert that may have come with your stockpot allows you to reserve the cooking water when you strain the noodles for rinsing. Then, just before serving, quickly dip them back into the hot water until they're reheated.

simple miso ramen

This ramen is as straightforward as it gets, with a rich, flavorful broth that supports the noodles. I encourage you to take liberties with the adornments—I've added a few very simple ones here. The one rule is to use a light hand. Ramen shouldn't be laden with toppings, or you'll end up with a wet mound. Let the broth and the noodles do their magic, then finesse it at the table, adding heat or salt to suit personal preferences. Be sure to play around with some of the condiments (see pages 237 to 247)—the *rayu* and seasoned oils and togarashi make eating ramen more exciting and delicious. If you're up for the challenge, give homemade ramen noodles a try. SERVES 4

1½ quarts Vegetarian Dashi (page 215)

2 tablespoons light-colored miso paste

2 teaspoons toasted sesame oil, Chili Oil (page 237), or Rayu (page 238)

2 tablespoons soy sauce, plus more for garnish

1 teaspoon fine sea salt

1 cup mung bean sprouts

8 ounces dried or 12 ounces fresh ramen noodles (page 232 or 235)

Two 2-inch squares toasted nori

3 scallions, white and green parts, thinly sliced

1 cup cubed silken tofu

4 large boiled eggs, molten or firm yolks (optional; page 224)

Garlic Chips (page 243), for optional garnish

Frizzled Shallots or Scallions (page 244), for optional garnish

Rayu (page 238), Chili Oil (page 237), or Chili-Bean Oil (page 240), for optional garnish

Togarashi Blend (page 245), for optional garnish

• Bring the dashi to a bare simmer in a stockpot.

• In a large glass or measuring cup, or the plastic cup that usually comes with an immersion blender, combine the miso, oil, and about ½ cup of the dashi. Puree with an immersion blender until smooth. (Alternatively, puree in a blender.) Stir the mixture back into the rest of the dashi. Add the soy sauce and salt and taste, adding more salt if needed. (It should be strongly flavored, but you can always pass more soy sauce at the table.) Keep at a bare simmer, covered, until ready to serve.

• Meanwhile, bring a pot of salted water to boil. Place the sprouts in a sieve, dunk them into the cooking water to quickly blanch them for about 10 seconds, then immediately lift them out and rinse under cold water. Reserve the boiling water.

• Add the noodles to the boiling water, in a strainer basket or the pasta insert that comes with your stockpot if you have one, and cook until tender, usually 4 to 7 minutes for dried, or according to the package instructions, or 60 to 90 seconds for fresh. Lift out the noodles, reserving the cooking water, and rinse the noodles thoroughly under cold running water in order to remove excess starch. Quickly dunk them back into the hot water to reheat. Divide among four bowls.

• Just before serving, wave the nori squares over the flame of a gas burner a few times, until the corners curl and they turn crisp, or roast under a broiler, flipping periodically. Slice into thin strips with a chef's knife, or crumble with your fingers.

• Arrange the scallions, sprouts, and tofu over the noodles in each bowl, then ladle piping hot broth over each serving. Top with the nori strips or crumbles. Add a soft egg or a halved hard-boiled one, if using, to each bowl and serve, passing the garnishes of your choice at the table.

spring ramen

This bowl features juicy sweet snap peas and the delicate, sharp flavor of shaved raw asparagus in a light broth that's brightened with lemon zest and fresh ginger. It also incorporates a streamlined kombu-soaking step, so that the dashi doesn't need to be prepared in advance. SERVES 4

8 ounces asparagus

4 dried shiitake mushrooms

2 plump garlic cloves, smashed

9 cups water

Four 2-inch squares kombu

2 tablespoons light-colored miso paste

1 teaspoon fine sea salt

4 ounces sugar snap peas

8 ounces dried or 12 ounces fresh ramen noodles (page 232 or 235)

Two 2-inch squares toasted nori

4 large boiled eggs, molten or firm yolks (optional; page 224)

4 pinches of freshly grated lemon zest

Pounded Ginger Pulp (page 247) or freshly grated ginger, to taste

1 cup Frizzled Scallions (page 244)

Toasted sesame oil, for garnish

• Snap off the tough ends of the asparagus and set the top parts aside. Combine the tough asparagus ends, mushrooms, garlic, and water in a stockpot or saucepan and bring to a boil. Reduce the heat and simmer for 20 minutes. Add the kombu, remove from the heat, and let stand for 30 minutes. Strain out and discard the solids and return the broth to the stockpot.

• In a tall glass or measuring cup, or the plastic cup that usually comes with an immersion blender, combine the miso and a ladleful of the hot broth. Puree thoroughly with an immersion blender until smooth. (Alternatively, puree in a blender.) Pour the mixture into the stockpot with the rest of the broth and bring to a bare simmer. Add the salt and taste, adding more salt as necessary. Keep covered over low heat until ready to serve.

- Use a vegetable peeler to shave the asparagus spears into ribbons. It's easiest to do this by laying them flat on a cutting board, and using a Y peeler.

- Bring another saucepan of salted water to boil and prepare an ice bath. Remove the fibrous strings from the snap peas: Pinch one end and pull along the straight edge of the pea as if it's a zipper. Once the water comes to a boil, add the snap peas and blanch for 90 seconds. Use a slotted spoon to transfer the peas to the ice bath. Reserve the boiling water.

- Add the noodles to the boiling water, in a strainer basket or the pasta insert that comes with your stockpot, if you have one, and cook until tender, usually 4 to 7 minutes for dried, (or according to the package instructions), or 60 to 90 seconds for fresh. Lift out the noodles, reserving the cooking water and rinse the noodles thoroughly under cold running water in order to remove excess starch. Quickly dunk them back into the hot water to reheat. Divide among four bowls.

- Just before serving, wave the nori squares over the flame of a gas burner a few times, until the corners curl and they turn crisp, or roast under a broiler, flipping periodically. Slice into thin strips with a chef's knife, or crumble with your fingers.

- Arrange the shaved asparagus, snap peas, and egg halves, if using, over the noodles in each bowl. Add a pinch of lemon zest and a scant teaspoon of ginger pulp or a few gratings of ginger to each bowl, then cover with the piping hot broth. Divide the frizzled scallions on top, garnish each serving with a few drops of sesame oil and the nori, and serve immediately.

vegetarian kimchi ramen

SOFT TOFU, FRIZZLED SCALLIONS, TENDER GREENS

I'm sometimes reluctant to give up so much of my precious homemade kim-chi to one recipe, but this ramen is worth it. It's tangy, rich comfort food, with deep earthy flavor from shiitake mushrooms and richness from a generous pour of toasted sesame oil. It's finished with soft pockets of tofu and salty wisps of frizzled scallions, and it will fortify and revive you during the coldest part of the winter. Using well-fermented kimchi makes a big difference, and homemade is preferable, especially because it yields the necessary amount of kimchi brine. Homemade kimchi should be at least a month old; taste store-bought to make sure it tastes tangy and funky. And if using store-bought, be sure to read the ingredients carefully to make sure it doesn't contain any fish or shrimp prod-ucts. SERVES 4

1 tablespoon neutral-tasting oil

1 tablespoon toasted sesame oil

1 large white onion, cut into thin strips

2 cups drained, very fermented Napa Cabbage Kimchi (page 227) or store-bought, chopped

5 cups water

½ cup kimchi brine

Four 2-inch squares kombu

6 dried shiitake mushrooms

1½ teaspoons fine sea salt

Pinch of sugar (optional)

8 ounces dried or 12 ounces fresh ramen noodles (page 232 or 235)

8 ounces soft tofu (about half of a 14-ounce container)

2 cups loosely packed trimmed tender greens and fresh herbs, such as watercress, baby spinach, or arugula, and basil or cilantro, or a combination

1 cup Frizzled Scallions (page 244)

2 tablespoons toasted sesame seeds

• Heat the oil and sesame oil in a saucepan or Dutch oven over medium heat. Add the onion and cook, stirring periodically, until just softened, 3 to 5 minutes. Add the chopped kimchi and cook, stirring for 1 minute until fragrant, then pour in the water and kimchi brine. Bring to a

boil. Remove from the heat, add the kombu and dried mushrooms, cover the pot, and let stand for 45 minutes.

• Remove the kombu and mushrooms, squeezing them to extract as much liquid as possible. Reserve the mushrooms and discard the kombu. Trim the stems off the mushrooms and discard them. Slice the mushroom caps into thin strips and add them back to the kimchi broth. Stir in the salt, taste, and add additional salt and a pinch of sugar if needed. Keep covered over low heat until ready to serve.

• Bring another saucepan of salted water to boil. Add the noodles, in a strainer basket or the pasta insert that comes with your stockpot, if you have one, and cook until tender, usually 4 to 7 minutes for dried (or according to the package instructions), or 60 to 90 seconds for fresh. Lift out the noodles, reserving the cooking water, and thoroughly rinse the noodles under cold running water in order to remove excess starch. Quickly dunk them back into the hot water to reheat. Divide among four bowls.

• Use a spoon to arrange small scoops of the soft tofu over the noodles in each bowl. Ladle the hot kimchi broth over each serving. Top with the tender greens and fresh herbs, frizzled scallions, and sesame seeds and serve immediately.

VARIATION To make this dish extra rich, add a poached egg (page 226) to each bowl just before serving.

kimchi brine

Kimchi brine is the liquid that accumulates with the kimchi as it ferments. Holding the kimchi in place with your hand or a slotted spoon, simply pour it out of the jar into a bowl or liquid measuring cup. You can also extract it from the kimchi itself by gathering it in your hands and giving it a gentle squeeze over a bowl or liquid measuring cup.

summer ramen

Corncobs provide a clear, summery corn flavor in this broth, which pairs beautifully with the kombu and the spiciness of fresh ginger. That summery flavor gets reinforced with raw corn kernels, ripe tomatoes, and a handful of basil at the very end. Definitely cook the eggs to a soft or molten yolk, which thickens the broth slightly when you stir it into the soup. SERVES 4

3 ears corn, husked

1 white or yellow onion, coarsely chopped

3 plump garlic cloves, smashed

½ ounce fresh ginger (1 thumb-sized piece), peeled and sliced into thin rounds

10 cups water

Four 2-inch squares kombu

1 teaspoon fine sea salt

8 ounces dried or 12 ounces fresh ramen noodles (page 232 or 235)

½ cup halved cherry tomatoes

4 large boiled eggs, molten yolks (optional; page 224)

½ cup fresh basil leaves, coarsely chopped

2 scallions, green and white parts, thinly sliced on the bias

Rayu (page 238) or Chili Oil (page 237), for serving

Togarashi Blend (page 245 or store-bought), for serving

• Cut the kernels off the corn: Place each corncob in the middle of a big cutting board. You can hold each piece upright or on its side. Using a sturdy chef's knife, cut downward or across to remove strips of kernels, rotating the cob as needed until you've worked all the way around the cob. Reserve the kernels.

• Place the stripped ears in a saucepan with the onion, garlic, ginger, and the water. Bring to a boil, reduce the heat to low, cover the pan partially, and simmer for 25 minutes. Add the kombu and remove from the heat. Cover and let stand for 20 minutes. Strain the broth and discard the solids, wipe out the saucepan, and then return the strained broth to the saucepan. Add the salt and taste, adding additional salt if needed. Let stand, covered, over low heat until ready to serve.

• Bring another saucepan of salted water to boil. Add the noodles, in a strainer basket or the pasta insert that comes with your stockpot, if you have one, and cook until tender, usually 4 to 7 minutes for dried (or according to the package instructions), or 60 to 90 seconds for fresh. Lift out the noodles, reserving the cooking water, and thoroughly rinse the noodles under cold running water in order to remove excess starch. Quickly dunk them back into the hot water to reheat. Divide among four bowls.

• Divide the tomatoes, reserved corn kernels, and eggs, if serving, over the noodles in each bowl. Cover each serving with the hot broth and scatter the basil and scallions on top. Serve immediately, passing the condiments at the table.

autumn ramen

BRUSSELS SPROUTS, ROASTED MUSHROOMS, CHILI BROTH

This spicy ramen broth is enriched with soy milk, which gives it a luxurious, creamy body but without any heaviness. Be sure to use an unflavored soy milk, and check the ingredients—the best store-bought soy milks only contain whole soybeans and water. The simple toppings—juicy roasted mushrooms, raw Brussels sprouts leaves, cubes of firm tofu, and crunchy sprouts—offer lots of contrast, but are mellow enough to let the good broth shine. SERVES 4

1 pound mixed mushrooms, such as shiitake, oyster, cremini, and white button, trimmed or torn into pieces about ½-inch thick

2 tablespoons neutral-tasting oil

¾ teaspoon fine sea salt

¼ teaspoon freshly ground black pepper

Pinch of red pepper flakes

1½ quarts Vegetarian Dashi (page 215)

3 to 4 dried whole chilies or 1 tablespoon red pepper flakes

5 garlic cloves, peeled and smashed

1 cup unflavored, good-quality soy milk

3 tablespoons light-colored miso paste

4 ounces Brussels sprouts (8 to 10 small ones)

8 ounces dried or 12 ounces fresh ramen noodles (page 232 or 235)

14 ounces firm tofu, blotted dry and cut into ¾-inch cubes

1 cup tender sprouts, shoots, or microgreens

Rayu (page 238), Chili Oil (page 237), or Chili-Bean Oil (page 240), for serving

Togarashi Blend (page 245 or store-bought), for serving

• Preheat the oven to 425°F.

• Divide the mushrooms between two baking sheets. Drizzle with the oil and sprinkle with ¼ teaspoon salt, the black pepper, and red pepper flakes. Use your hands to toss so that the mushrooms are well coated. Roast for 20 to 30 minutes, stirring periodically, until the mushrooms are tender and crispy around the edges.

- Meanwhile, combine the dashi, chilies, and garlic in a saucepan. Bring to a simmer, then cover, remove from the heat, and let steep for 30 minutes. Strain out and discard the solids and return the broth to the saucepan.

- In a large glass or measuring cup, or the tall plastic cup that usually comes with an immersion blender, combine the soy milk and the miso. Puree with an immersion blender until smooth. (Alternatively, puree in a blender.) Pour the mixture into the broth and bring to a bare simmer. Stir in the remaining ½ teaspoon salt and taste for balance, adding more salt if needed.

- Trim the root ends off of the Brussels sprouts. Gently separate the leaves, and halve or quarter the firm cores.

- Meanwhile, bring a saucepan of water to boil and salt it generously. Add the noodles, in a strainer basket or the pasta insert that comes with your stockpot if you have one, and cook until tender, usually 4 to 7 minutes for dried (or according to the package instructions), or 60 to 90 seconds for fresh. Lift out the noodles, reserving the cooking water, and rinse the noodles thoroughly under cold running water in order to remove excess starch. Quickly dunk them back into the hot water to reheat. Divide among four bowls.

- Divide the roasted mushrooms, tofu, and Brussels sprouts over the noodles. Ladle the hot broth over each serving and top with the tender sprouts. Serve immediately, passing the condiments of your choice at the table.

ginger-miso ramen

KABOCHA SQUASH, AVOCADO, CABBAGE

One great thing about the winter squash kabocha (a.k.a. Japanese pumpkin) is that it doesn't need to be peeled; the skin turns silky when cooked. Use peeled butternut squash, acorn squash, pumpkin, or even sweet potato if you're unable to find kabocha. While kabocha has legions of fans, cabbage is still an underappreciated gem of a vegetable, and a single head has a deceptively large yield. It's also a treat in the winter, when the crop freeze crystallizes its sugars and makes for a delectably sweet harvest. Here it's served in a rich, bright, gingery ramen broth and accompanied by a few savory slices of avocado. Substitute a soft-boiled egg for the avocado if you wish. SERVES 4

12 ounces kabocha squash, seeded and cut into ¾-inch cubes (about 2 cups)

2 quarts Vegetarian Dashi (page 215)

4 scallions, green and white parts, thinly sliced

2 tablespoons neutral-tasting oil

2 tablespoons light-colored miso paste

1½ tablespoons freshly grated ginger

2 teaspoons rice vinegar

1 teaspoon fine sea salt

8 ounces dried or 12 ounces fresh ramen noodles (page 232 or 235)

Two 2-inch squares toasted nori

1 avocado, quartered and sliced into thin wedges

1 cup thinly sliced green, savoy, or Napa cabbage

Rayu (page 238), Chili Oil (page 237), or Chili-Bean Oil (page 240), for serving

Togarashi Blend (page 245 or store-bought), for serving

• Bring a pot of salted water to boil. Reduce to a simmer, add the squash, and cook until just tender, about 5 minutes. Fish it out with a spider skimmer or slotted spoon and set aside. Return the water to the stove.

• Bring the dashi to a bare simmer in another saucepan.

• In a large glass or measuring cup, or the plastic cup that usually comes with an immersion blender, combine the scallions, oil, miso, ginger, vinegar, and a few ladlefuls of the dashi. Puree with an immersion blender. (Alternatively, puree in a blender.) Pour the mixture into the saucepan with the rest of the dashi and bring to a bare simmer. Add the salt and taste, adding more salt if necessary, and let stand, covered, over low heat until ready to assemble the ramen.

• Return the water to a boil. Add the noodles, in a strainer basket or the pasta insert that comes with your stockpot if you have one, and cook until tender, usually 4 to 7 minutes for dried (or according to the package instructions), or 60 to 90 seconds for fresh. Lift out the noodles, reserving the cooking water, and rinse the noodles thoroughly under cold running water in order to remove excess starch. Quickly dunk them back into the hot water to reheat. Divide among four bowls.

• Just before serving, wave the nori squares over the flame of a gas burner a few times, until the corners curl and they turn crisp, or roast under a broiler, flipping periodically. Slice into thin strips with a chef's knife, or crumble with your fingers.

• Divide the squash, avocado, and cabbage over the noodles in each bowl. Ladle piping hot broth over each serving, garnish with the nori, and serve, passing the condiments of your choice at the table.

mushroom soba noodles

SPICY DASHI, SPRING SHOOTS, SOFT TOFU

Tender shoots and sprouts play off savory, meaty mushrooms in this spicy bowl, which is an excellent way to showcase good mushrooms. Your grocery store may have a chef's sampler pack of different varieties, or better yet, see if your farmers' market includes a mushroom forager. And of course you can mix and match whatever mushrooms are available: oysters, trumpets, clamshells, maitakes— the more the better. Mirin is a sweet Japanese cooking wine made from rice, similar to sake but with a low alcohol content; it can be found at most grocery stores, but for best-quality mirin, head to Japanese markets. SERVES 4

Four 2-inch squares kombu

3 dried shiitake mushrooms

½ ounce fresh ginger (1 thumb-sized piece), peeled and sliced into thin rounds

3 garlic cloves, smashed

¼ teaspoon red pepper flakes, or more to taste

7 cups hot but not boiling water

1 tablespoon neutral-tasting oil

8 ounces mixed mushrooms (see above), sliced or torn into bite-sized pieces

1½ teaspoons fine sea salt

¼ cup mirin

2 tablespoons soy sauce

3 bundles dried soba noodles (about 10.5 ounces)

7 ounces soft tofu (about half of a 14-ounce package), drained

1 cup mixed shoots and sprouts, such as sunflower sprouts, pea shoots, broccoli sprouts, or microgreens, for garnish

Pounded Ginger Pulp (page 247), or freshly grated ginger, for garnish

• To make dashi, place the kombu, dried shiitakes, sliced ginger, garlic, and red pepper flakes in a 2- or 3-quart saucepan or heat-safe pitcher or liquid measuring cup. Cover with the hot water. Top with a lid or plate and let steep for 20 minutes.

• Heat a skillet over medium-high heat and add the oil. Once hot, add the mushrooms, spreading them in an even single layer, and sprinkle with a pinch of salt (depending on the size of your skillet, it may be necessary to cook the mushrooms in two batches, adding more oil as needed). Cook, disturbing the pan as little as possible so as to encourage caramelization, for anywhere from 3 to 7 minutes depending on how delicate or sturdy the mushrooms are, just until they start to go limp and look juicy. Remove from the heat.

• Pick out the dried mushrooms from the dashi, gently squeezing them over the broth, and set aside. Strain the dashi into a saucepan, discarding the rest of the solids. Bring to a simmer and stir in the salt, mirin, and soy sauce. Taste and adjust seasonings as necessary. Keep covered, over low heat, until ready to serve.

• Trim the stems off the rehydrated shiitake mushrooms and discard them, then thinly slice the caps. Add to the cooked mushrooms.

• Bring a saucepan of salted water to a gentle boil. Add the noodles in a strainer basket or the pasta insert that comes with your stockpot, if you have one, and cook until tender, usually 4 to 7 minutes or according to the package instructions. Lift out the noodles, reserving the cooking water, and thoroughly rinse the noodles under cold running water in order to remove excess starch. Quickly dunk them back into the hot water to reheat. Divide among four bowls.

• Divide the mushrooms over the noodles in each bowl. Use a spoon to divide small scoops of the tofu into the bowls. Cover each serving with the hot broth and then garnish with the shoots and a spoonful of ginger pulp or few gratings of ginger. Serve immediately.

vegetarian curry laksa

COCONUT, GREEN BEANS, TOMATOES, PEANUTS

This fragrant, vibrantly colored, rich bowl called *laksa* can be thought of as the Malaysian street-food counterpart to Japanese ramen. Authentic, non-vegetarian versions call for seafood in most of the primary components. My vegetarian *laksa* is a little lighter, but still has a good deal of body from the coconut milk and a heady, fragrant spiciness from curry paste. I encourage you to make your own curry paste—the recipe that follows is modeled after a fragrant Malaysian curry paste, and the most complicated part about it is sourcing the galangal, fresh turmeric, and lemongrass. But you can certainly substitute store-bought curry paste—just check to make sure all the ingredients are vegetarian. Brown rice vermicelli noodles make a great substitute for the wheat noodles used here. SERVES 4

2 tablespoons coconut oil

½ cup Red Curry Paste (page 63), or one 4-ounce can store-bought red curry paste

3 cups vegetable stock, preferably homemade (see page 219)

1¾ cups coconut milk (one 14-ounce can)

1 branch fresh curry leaves (optional)

1 teaspoon fine sea salt

1 teaspoon sugar

2 cups mung bean sprouts

4 ounces green beans, stem ends trimmed

8 ounces dried or 12 ounces fresh ramen noodles (page 232 or 235)

1 cup shredded savoy or green cabbage

4 large boiled eggs, firm yolks (page 224), halved

½ cup quartered cherry tomatoes

½ cup coarsely chopped roasted peanuts, for garnish

1 cup coarsely chopped fresh cilantro leaves and tender stems, for garnish

Lime wedges, for serving

• Heat the coconut oil in a saucepan over low heat. Add the curry paste and cook, stirring frequently, until darkened, very fragrant, and caramelized, 20 to 30 minutes. Add a big splash of the vegetable stock and use a wooden spoon to scrape up any browned bits from the bottom of the pan, then add the rest of the stock, the coconut milk, and curry leaves, if using. Bring to

a simmer and cook gently for 20 minutes. Add the salt and sugar, then taste and adjust the seasonings as necessary. Remove from the heat.

- Bring a saucepan of water to boil and salt it lightly. Prepare an ice-water bath.

- Place the bean sprouts in a sieve and dip them into the boiling water for 10 seconds. Lift out of the water and immediately rinse under cold running water.

- Using the same boiling water, blanch the green beans for about 1 minute, until just tender (test by piercing one with a paring knife). Use a spider skimmer or slotted spoon to transfer the green beans to the ice-water bath, reserving the boiling water, then drain the green beans.

- Return the water to a boil. Add the noodles, in a strainer basket or the pasta insert that comes with your stockpot if you have one, and cook until tender, usually 4 to 7 minutes for dried (or according to the package instructions), or 60 to 90 seconds for fresh. Lift out the noodles, reserving the cooking water, and thoroughly rinse the noodles under cold running water in order to remove excess starch. Quickly dunk them back into the hot water to reheat. Divide among four bowls.

- Top the noodles in each bowl with the bean sprouts, green beans, cabbage, eggs, and tomatoes. Divide the broth among the bowls. Garnish with the peanuts and cilantro and serve immediately, with the lime wedges on the side.

curry leaves

Used primarily as an aromatic in many cuisines of the world, curry leaves add an unmistakable, somewhat lemony flavor to soup-based bowls. They bear no relation to curry powder. Small branches of fresh curry leaves are increasingly available at Western grocery stores, alongside the other fresh herbs in the produce department. Or more reliably, you can find them at Indian groceries and many Asian markets that cater to Malaysian and Indonesian clienteles where they're sometimes sold from the freezer. If using frozen curry leaves, don't bother thawing them first; add them directly to what you're cooking.

red curry paste

To activate some of the flavors, and for a more sensory experience, toast the whole spices in a dry skillet over medium-low heat until aromatic, just a minute or two. And if you want a workout, make this curry paste in a big mortar and pestle. MAKES ABOUT ½ CUP

1 ounce dried hot red chilies (3 or 4)

5 whole black peppercorns

2 whole cloves

1 tablespoon whole coriander seeds

1 teaspoon whole cumin seeds, toasted

½ teaspoon fennel seeds

2 medium shallots

½ ounce peeled galangal or ginger (about a thumb-sized knob)

½ ounce peeled fresh turmeric (about a thumb-sized knob)

3 garlic cloves

2 stalks lemongrass, white parts only, thinly sliced

• Trim the stems off the chilies. Combine with the peppercorns, cloves, and the coriander, cumin, and fennel seeds in a spice mill or a mini food processor until powdery. If using a spice mill, transfer to a food processor along with the remaining ingredients and pulse until a paste forms. If using a small food processor, add the remaining ingredients and process until a paste forms. Add water by the tablespoon to get the mixture moving if necessary. In an airtight container, the paste will keep for a few days in the refrigerator or for up to 3 months in the freezer.

gado-gado with wheat noodles

COCONUT-PEANUT DRESSING, FRIED POTATOES, BOILED VEGETABLES

Gado-Gado, the popular Indonesian boiled vegetable salad, is a component-heavy dish, but worth every ounce of effort. The wheat noodles bump it up from a side dish to a filling main and its rich and hearty peanut sauce can be repurposed for other salads or as a dipping sauce for fritters and dumplings. Since your kitchen will get a workout, it's best to approach this recipe with a willingness to wash dishes as you go. Try substituting cashew butter for the peanut butter.

SERVES 4

5 tablespoons natural, chunky peanut butter

3 plump garlic cloves, minced

1 or 2 small hot chili peppers, such as serrano, seeded and finely minced

3 tablespoons brown sugar

3/4 cup coconut milk

1/2 cup water

3/4 teaspoon kosher salt, plus more as needed

Zest of 1 lime

1 tablespoon fresh lime juice

Peanut oil, for frying

2 medium Yukon gold potatoes (6 to 8 ounces total), sliced into 1/2-inch-thick disks

3 medium shallots or 1 small onion, sliced into very thin rings

6 cups shredded crisp lettuce, such as butter leaf, Boston, romaine, or iceberg

5 ounces dried or 8 ounces fresh ramen noodles (page 232 or 235)

1 large carrot (6 to 8 ounces), or equivalent weight in smaller carrots, peeled and cut on the bias into 1/2-inch-thick disks

4 ounces green beans, trimmed and cut into 1/2-inch lengths

3 large boiled eggs, firm yolks (page 224), cut into chunks

1/2 cup coarsely chopped fresh mint, for garnish

1/2 cup coarsely chopped fresh cilantro, for garnish

1/2 cup finely chopped peanuts, for garnish

• Combine the peanut butter, garlic, chilies, and brown sugar in a medium saucepan and whisk until combined. Gently stir in the coconut milk, then place over medium heat and cook, stirring frequently, until very aromatic and the coconut oil begins to separate on the surface, 6 to 8 minutes. Stir in the water and salt and cook for another 3 to 5 minutes, until thickened slightly.

The dressing should be the consistency of glue. If too thick, stir in additional water 1 tablespoon at a time; if too thin, cook for a few minutes more. Remove from the heat and stir in the lime zest and juice. You should have about 1¾ cups dressing. Let cool completely. The dressing can be made up to 3 days in advance and stored in an airtight container in the refrigerator.

• Pour ½ inch oil into a deep skillet or saucepan and heat over a medium-high heat. Test the temperature by dipping in a potato disk—there should be an active sizzle. When the oil is hot enough, add the potatoes and fry, flipping them frequently, until tender and golden brown on both sides, 3 to 5 minutes per batch. Use a slotted spoon to transfer the cooked potatoes to a paper towel– or paper bag–lined plate to drain and cool. Sprinkle with a pinch of salt. Reserve the oil and keep it over the heat.

• Reduce the heat to medium, add the shallots to the oil, and cook, stirring frequently, until reddish brown and crisp, 10 to 15 minutes. Watch carefully, as they easily burn. Use the slotted spoon to transfer to the lined plate to drain and cool. Sprinkle with a pinch or two of salt.

• Place the lettuce in a large serving bowl.

• Bring a saucepan of water to boil and salt it generously. Add the noodles in a strainer basket or the pasta insert that comes with your stockpot, if you have one, and cook until tender, usually 4 to 7 minutes for dried (or according to the package instructions), or 60 to 90 seconds for fresh. Lift out the noodles, reserving the cooking water, and thoroughly rinse the noodles under cold running water to remove excess starch. Drain thoroughly, then add to the bowl with the lettuce.

• Add the carrots to the boiling water and cook until just tender, about 2 minutes, then transfer to a colander—again reserving the cooking water, keeping it over the heat—and rinse until cool. Drain thoroughly, blot gently with a kitchen towel to sop up as much water as possible, and add to the bowl. Add the green beans to the boiling water and cook until just tender, 60 to 90 seconds, then transfer to the colander and rinse until cool. Drain thoroughly, blot gently with a kitchen towel to sop up as much water as possible, and add to the bowl.

• To serve, add the potatoes and eggs to the serving bowl. Pour in about 1 cup of the dressing, toss gently with your hands, making sure that everything is well coated, and taste. You may want to add more dressing—you need a fair amount so that the flavors are bold. Divide among four bowls, garnish with the fried shallots, mint, cilantro, and peanuts, and serve immediately.

cold kimchi noodles

SOBA NOODLES, PICKLED APPLE, BASIL

I've long loved the combination of chilies and sweet fruit, and that prompted this unorthodox cold kimchi noodle salad, made with threads of quick-pickled apple woven throughout the noodles. Fresh basil and a host of Asian pantry staples—soy sauce, scallions, toasted sesame oil—make this a flavorful noodle bowl with lots of complexity. Substitute udon or somen noodles for the soba if you like. SERVES 4

2 apples, peeled if desired and cored

5 tablespoons rice vinegar, plus more as needed

3 tablespoons plus 1 teaspoon sugar

1½ teaspoons fine sea salt

2/3 cup very hot tap water

3 bundles (about 11.5 ounces) dried soba noodles

2 cups Napa Cabbage or Bok Choy Kimchi, preferably homemade (page 227)

2 tablespoons neutral-tasting oil

2 tablespoons dark soy sauce

1 tablespoon *gochujang* (see page 37)

1 scant tablespoon toasted sesame oil

3 scallions, white and pale green parts, thinly sliced

¼ cup sliced fresh chives (cut into 1-inch lengths), for garnish

3 tablespoons thinly sliced fresh basil, for garnish

• Slice the apples into thin matchsticks: With a flat surface down, cut into wedges about ⅛ inch thick. Stack these wedges on top of one another and carefully cut into ⅛-inch-wide matchsticks.

• Whisk together the vinegar, 2 tablespoons of the sugar, the salt, and hot water until the sugar and salt dissolve. Combine with the apples in a nonreactive container and let stand for at least 30 minutes, or up to 5 hours.

• Bring a saucepan of water to boil and salt it generously. Add the noodles in a strainer basket or the pasta insert that comes with your stockpot, if you have one, and cook until tender, usually 4 to 7 minutes, or according to the package instructions. Lift out the noodles, reserving the cooking water, and thoroughly rinse the noodles under cold running water in order to remove excess starch. Drain thoroughly.

• Gently squeeze the kimchi over a large bowl to extract the brine and reserve the brine. Coarsely chop the kimchi. Add additional brine (or rice vinegar) to the bowl as needed to measure 3 tablespoons.

• Combine the kimchi, kimchi brine, oil, soy sauce, *gochujang*, sesame oil, and remaining 1 tablespoon plus 1 teaspoon sugar, stirring to combine. Taste for balance, adding salt, soy sauce, sugar, or additional *gochujang* if needed. (The sauce should be full-flavored, as it will dilute when it's added to the noodles.) Drain the apples, then add them, the scallions, and the noodles to the kimchi mixture, tossing gently with your hands or tongs to coat. Garnish with the chives and basil, and serve.

cold ramen

In cold ramen, toppings are arranged over cooked, chilled noodles, and then served with a very flavorful, sweet, soy-based dressing (called *tare*) that can be poured over the bowl or used as a dipping sauce for individual bites, similar to Zaru Soba (page 70). It's a great way to showcase good ramen noodles if you have them—and the perfect opportunity to make your own. The slurpy, stretchy qualities are an excellent contrast to all the other juicy, cool, and crunchy textures in this summertime bowl. Swiss chard has a succulent, luxurious quality, and I love it against the crunchy cabbage. A liberal sprinkling of togarashi is crucial. Substitute avocado slices for the boiled egg to make this vegan. SERVES 4

¼ cup soy sauce

2 tablespoons rice vinegar

1 tablespoon honey

2 teaspoons molasses

1 teaspoon toasted sesame oil

1 big bunch Swiss chard, stems removed and discarded or reserved for another use (about 12 ounces)

8 ounces dried or 12 ounces fresh ramen noodles (page 232 or 235)

4 large boiled eggs, firm yolks (page 224)

Four 2-inch squares toasted nori

1 cup ripe cherry tomatoes, quartered

1 cup finely shredded cabbage

2 scallions, green and white parts, thinly sliced

2 tablespoons minced fresh chives

Togarashi Blend (page 245 or store-bought), for serving

• Make the dressing by whisking together the soy sauce, vinegar, honey, molasses, and sesame oil. Refrigerate until chilled, at least 30 minutes but ideally a few hours.

• Bring a pot of water to boil and prepare an ice-water bath. Add the chard to the boiling water and cook for 30 to 90 seconds, until wilted. Use a spider skimmer to transfer the chard to the ice-water bath, reserving the cooking water. Once the chard is cool, drain and squeeze dry, then coarsely chop. Return the water to the heat.

- Add the noodles to the boiling water and cook until tender, usually 4 to 7 minutes for dried (or according to the package instructions), or 60 to 90 seconds for fresh. Drain and thoroughly rinse under cold running water, then drain thoroughly.

- Slice the eggs into thin rings. Wave the nori squares over the flame of a gas burner a few times, until the corners curl and they turn crisp, or roast under a broiler, flipping periodically.

- Divide the noodles among four bowls. Top with the chard, tomatoes, cabbage, and egg. Sprinkle with the scallions and chives, then crumble a square of toasted nori over each serving. Pour about 1½ tablespoons of the dressing over each serving (alternatively, serve it on the side as a dipping sauce, in small bowls so diners can dip individual bites in the sauce as they go). Serve, passing the togarashi and additional dressing as needed at the table.

zaru soba

Zaru soba is a light and simple Japanese side dish intended for balmy weather. Traditionally, cold cooked soba noodles are served on a bamboo platter called a *zaru*, garnished minimally with wasabi, grated daikon radish, and some sliced scallions, and dipped into the thin, flavorful sauce (which is available premade at Japanese grocery stores; it most often contains bonito flakes). This version is plumped into more of a main meal but retains its refreshing qualities. Thin ribbons of cold cucumber mingle with the noodles, avocado adds creaminess, and ripe, juicy mango contributes a refreshing brightness. Substitute summer fruits like nectarines or peaches for the mango if they're in season. This is a great dish to pack for picnics—put all the components into separate containers, pass bowls around, and let everyone dish up their own. Store it on lots of ice. SERVES 4

1 cup sake

1½ cups Vegetarian Dashi (page 215)

½ cup soy sauce

¼ cup sugar

Scant ½ teaspoon ground wasabi powder

3 bundles (about 11.5 ounces) dried soba noodles

2 Persian or Kirby cucumbers, peeled if desired

1 mango

1 avocado

Two 2-inch squares toasted nori

¼ cup finely grated peeled daikon radish

• Place the sake in a saucepan and bring to a simmer. Cook for about 2 minutes, to cook off most of the alcohol, then add the dashi, soy sauce, and sugar. Bring to a simmer and cook until the sugar is dissolved. Remove from the heat and let cool. Whisk together the wasabi powder and a spoonful of the sake mixture to make a paste, then stir the paste into the liquid in the saucepan. Store the dipping sauce in the refrigerator until thoroughly chilled, about 4 hours.

• Bring a pot of salted water to boil and prepare an ice-water bath. Add the soba noodles and cook until tender, usually 6 to 8 minutes or according to the package instructions. Drain, rinse

under cold running water, then plunge into the ice-water bath. Swish the noodles with your fingers to chill them as quickly as possible. Drain thoroughly and store in the refrigerator until ready to serve.

• If using Kirby cucumbers, slice them in half and scrape out the seeds with a spoon (there's no need to seed Persian cucumbers). Cut the cucumbers into long, thin strands using the julienne setting of a mandoline. Alternatively, shave the cucumbers into thin slabs with a vegetable peeler, then stack the slabs on top of each other and carefully cut into thin strands using a long, sharp knife.

• Peel the mango with a vegetable peeler. Then hold it upright on a cutting board, stem facing up, and, with a sharp knife, cut the flesh off from the two widest sides, getting as close to the pit as possible. Work your way around the pit, cutting long strips off. You'll be left with an oddly shaped pit that still has some fruit left on it; this is great for snacking. Lay the large pieces flat on the cutting board and cut them into thin wedges.

• Pit and peel the avocado and cut into wedges roughly the same width as the mango.

• Wave the nori squares over the flame of a gas burner a few times until they curl and the corners crisp, or roast under a broiler, flipping periodically. Stack the nori sheets on top of each other and, with a sharp knife, slice into the thinnest possible strips, or crumble them with your fingers.

• To serve, divide the noodles among four shallow bowls. Arrange the cucumber, mango, and avocado around the noodles. Place a mound of grated daikon and a little pile of shredded nori on each dish. Divide the dipping sauce between four small bowls. Use chopsticks to dip the noodles and toppings into the cold dipping sauce, bite by bite.

cashew-scallion noodles

CABBAGE, CUCUMBER, TOMATOES, HERBS

I love a rich, quietly vegan summer dish like this one. The cashew-scallion dressing is undeniably creamy, yet it's light and refreshing, with a hint of umami from the miso paste and some sharpness from the scallions. The starting point was cold peanut or sesame noodles, the Chinese restaurant standby, but I wanted to make it a bit more vegetal rather than nut-centric, with big, crunchy cubes of cabbage. Experiment with the vegetables: Try adding slivers of bell pepper, blanched broccoli rabe or broccoli, or swap in salted summer squash for the cucumber. Just don't skimp on the fresh herbs. SERVES 4

½ cup raw cashews, soaked overnight in cold water

3 scallions, white and green parts, cut into 1-inch pieces

1 to 2 tablespoons light-colored miso paste

1 tablespoon neutral-tasting oil

2 teaspoons rice vinegar

1 teaspoon fine sea salt

12 ounces dried soba, udon, or somen noodles

1 pound green or savoy cabbage (half a small-to-medium head)

1 medium cucumber

1 pint cherry tomatoes, halved or quartered

1 bunch watercress, tough stems removed

2 cups loosely packed fresh herbs such as mint, basil, or cilantro

¼ cup toasted cashews

• Drain and rinse the raw cashews, then combine them with the scallions, 1 tablespoon miso, the oil, vinegar, and ½ teaspoon of the salt in a food processor. Pulse until you have a chunky paste, scraping down the sides of the bowl as necessary. With the motor running, pour in 2 tablespoons water. Add more water as needed until the dressing has a pourable consistency. Taste, and add more salt or miso if needed.

• Bring a saucepan of water to boil and salt it generously. Break the noodles in half and add them to the water. Cook until tender, usually 4 to 7 minutes, or according to the package instructions. Drain and then rinse under cold running water until cool enough to handle. Drain thoroughly and transfer to a mixing bowl.

• Meanwhile, cut out the core of the cabbage, then cut the cabbage into ¾-inch cubes. Place in a colander. Peel the cucumber and cut it in half lengthwise, then scrape out the seeds with a spoon. Slice on the bias into half-moons about ¼ inch thick. Add to the colander with the cabbage. Toss well with the remaining ½ teaspoon salt and let stand for at least 15 minutes, then gently press dry.

• Add the salted vegetables to the noodles, along with the cherry tomatoes. Add about three quarters of the dressing and mix well with tongs to ensure that everything is well coated. Taste and add more dressing as needed.

• Divide the noodles among four bowls. Just before serving, top with the watercress, herbs, and toasted cashews.

black sesame noodle bowl

SHREDDED EGG, AVOCADO, SHALLOTS

For this noodle bowl, I took inspiration from Heidi Swanson's Black Sesame Otsu in *Super Natural Every Day*, in which a blanket of black sesame seeds is toasted until it smells heady, then pounded with a mortar and pestle and combined with some Asian pantry staples to make a thick, savory, and tangy dressing, here given a bit more punch with wasabi. Like other cold noodle dishes, this is a good dish for packing up, and in my experience has been wonderful on the beach. The shredded egg and wisps of radish incorporate into the noodles, the shallot brings crunch and zing, and the final drizzle of *kecap manis*—the Indonesian soy sauce— brings the whole bowl together in the most satisfying way. SERVES 4

¼ cup black sesame seeds

2 tablespoons neutral-tasting oil

5 teaspoons soy sauce

1 tablespoon rice vinegar

1 tablespoon brown sugar

½ teaspoon wasabi powder

¼ teaspoon fine sea salt

3 bundles (about 11.5 ounces) dried soba, udon, or somen noodles

2 medium shallots, minced

1 avocado

2 large boiled eggs, firm yolks (page 224)

8 small-to-medium radishes

4 cups tender greens, such as watercress, upland cress, baby arugula, or tatsoi

2 scallions, white and green parts, thinly sliced

Kecap manis (Indonesian soy sauce), for drizzling

• Place the sesame seeds in a dry skillet and set over medium-low heat. Toast, swirling the pan frequently, until fragrant—90 seconds to 2 minutes. Watch and smell carefully so that they don't burn. Transfer to a mortar and coarsely grind, then transfer to a mixing bowl. Add the oil, soy sauce, vinegar, brown sugar, wasabi, and salt, and whisk until thoroughly combined.

• Bring a saucepan of salted water to a gentle boil. Add the noodles and cook until tender, usually 4 to 7 minutes or according to the package instructions. Drain, rinse thoroughly under cold running water, then drain again thoroughly.

• Add the noodles and shallots to the bowl with the sauce and toss well, until the noodles are thoroughly coated. At this stage, the noodles can be transferred to an airtight container and kept in the fridge for up to 2 days. Bring to room temperature before serving.

• Quarter the avocado around the pit. Remove and peel the segments, then slice into thin strips. Peel the eggs and grate them using the large holes of a box grater. Slice the radishes into thin rounds. Stack the rounds on top of each other and slice into thin matchsticks.

• Divide the greens among four bowls, then top with the dressed noodles. Fan the avocado over the noodles in each bowl, then add a pile of the shredded egg, radishes, and scallions to each serving. Drizzle a bit of *kecap manis* over the avocado and serve.

zucchini soba noodles

SPINACH, WAKAME, TOASTED ALMONDS

Cold wilted spinach, zucchini, and specks of sweet, tender wakame (a sea vegetable, see page 32) all rest in a rich little pool of sweet-savory dashi in this juicy dish (the broth component here is more like an intensely flavored sauce—it doesn't submerge the noodles and other toppings). Opt for bunch spinach rather than the clamshell packs of baby spinach because the larger leaves and stems, when wilted, incorporate better into the dish—like slippery, succulent noodles. Toasted almonds round everything out here—definitely don't skip them—and freshly toasted, as always, are best for flavor and crunch. Beet greens and leaf amaranth make great substitutes for the spinach. SERVES 4

2 cups Vegetarian Dashi (page 215)

2 tablespoons mirin

1 tablespoon soy sauce

1½ teaspoons sugar

1¾ teaspoons fine sea salt

2 small zucchini (8 to 10 ounces total)

¼ cup wakame

1 big bunch mature spinach (12 to 16 ounces), well cleaned

3 bundles (about 11.5 ounces) dried soba, udon, or somen noodles

½ cup sliced almonds, toasted

• Combine the dashi, mirin, soy sauce, sugar, and ¾ teaspoon of the salt in a saucepan, stirring just until the sugar and salt dissolve. Remove from the heat and allow to cool, then transfer to the refrigerator to chill thoroughly, about 4 hours. The seasoned dashi can be prepared several days in advance and stored in an airtight container in the refrigerator.

• Using a mandoline, julienne the zucchini into long, very thin ribbons. Or to do this without a mandoline, use a vegetable peeler to cut the zucchini into long, thin slabs, then stack the slabs on top of one another and slice lengthwise into thin ribbons. Place in a colander and toss with the remaining 1 teaspoon salt. Let drain for 20 minutes, then squeeze to extract excess water.

• Cover the wakame with cold water and let stand for 5 minutes, until rehydrated. Drain and squeeze gently to extract excess liquid. If you purchased your wakame whole rather than pre-chopped, coarsely chop into bite-sized pieces.

• Bring a pot of water to a gentle boil and prepare an ice-water bath. Add the spinach to the boiling water and cook for 45 seconds to 1 minute, until wilted. Remove with a spider skimmer, reserving the cooking water, and plunge into the ice bath. Once cool, drain the spinach and squeeze out excess moisture.

• Return the pot of water to the heat. Add the noodles and cook until just tender, usually 4 to 7 minutes, or according to the package instructions. Drain, rinse under cold running water until cool, then drain again thoroughly.

• Divide the noodles among four bowls. Top each one with piles of the salted zucchini, wakame, and spinach, then sprinkle with the almonds. Pour ½ cup of the cold seasoned dashi over the noodles and vegetables in each bowl and serve.

pho, bibimbap, and other rice noodle and rice bowls

Rice is one of the oldest, if not the oldest, cultivated grains, dating back to at least 4000 BC, and many believe it to have been harvested prior to that. It grows all over the world and is a staple food for billions of people in hundreds of different cuisines. Ground to make rice flour and combined with starch and water, it's the basis of rice noodles, another staple of many Asian cuisines and an increasingly popular choice among gluten-averse Westerners.

Pho (pronounced "fuh") is a Vietnamese rice noodle soup, originally eaten for breakfast. This makes sense when you consider that the climate of Vietnam is tropical—imagine a steaming bowl of spiced soup as an invigorating start to the day, during its coolest hours. It's good at any meal, of course, and I particularly like to have vegetarian pho for dinner on the night before a race or a long morning run. It supplies me with just the kind of energy I need.

There are countless variations of pho, but some of its trademarks are a fragrant broth—flavored with such assertive aromatics as charred onion and ginger and with whole warm spices like star anise, clove, and cinnamon sticks—and the copious fresh herbs that are served alongside it at the table, among them cilantro, basil, and mint. Vegetarian pho is light and refreshing, an exercise in the balance of delicate flavors. It's also a bowl to be enjoyed with lots of garnishes and accompaniments to choose from, and these recipes list many options.

Another rice-based meal-in-a-bowl is bibimbap, the signature dish of Korea. It is essentially a rice bowl topped with an assortment of different cooked, raw, and pickled vegetables and proteins, and enriched with egg and a sweet chili sauce. Traditionally the hot, freshly cooked rice and toppings go into a *dolsot*, a Korean stone bowl that's preheated before serving and lightly brushed with oil. The dish is then rushed to the table, where an egg is cracked on top and vigorously folded in, cooking on contact with the hot elements. Besides functioning as a heat vessel, the *dolsot* crisps the rice, adding texture to the dish. To mimic this effect without one, I've included an optional step in the following recipes, a technique I first read about in Elaine Louie's *The Occasional Vegetarian*. Press the cooked rice into a hot, lightly greased skillet and leave it there to develop a crust. Then scoop it out with a spatula and divide it among the bowls, making sure that everyone gets some of the crispy part.

The first bibimbap recipe in this chapter is a basic one, laying the groundwork for a vegetarian adaptation of the dish. Those that follow are seasonal variations, all of which employ different flavor profiles and techniques for toppings. Bibimbap, with its blank-canvas versatility, is a tough dish not to love. You may find yourself cooking it often.

drink pairings for ramen, pho, and bibimbap

Pairing vegetarian ramen, pho, and bibimbap with drinks is a little different from pairing meat-based versions of those dishes, because vegetarian versions don't have the same fatty richness. Richer dishes can hold up to stronger drinks, but vegetarian ones require a bit more delicacy.

CRISP, REFRESHING BEERS

For the same reason that salty fried food tastes good with light beers, savory ramen goes very well with cold, crisp beers such as Kölsch, pilsner, and lager.

FRUITY AND SOUR BEERS

Citrusy wheat beers, such as a Belgian witbier, pair well with spicy ramen. Sour beers, like a German gose can also be an excellent pairing. A lightly sweet saison ale is also good, and one that has hints of warm spice pairs well with pho.

MEDIUM-BODIED ROSÉ AND WHITE WINES

These are my go-to wines for most of the bowls in this book. The rounded fruitiness of medium-bodied rosé is a good all-around pairing for miso and soy, ginger, and garlic flavor profiles, as well as for the fresh herbs in pho. Unoaked Chardonnays and Pinot Grigios often work in much the same way.

DRY CIDER

A good, very dry apple or pear cider is terrific with dishes like Vegetarian Kimchi Ramen (page 47) and any of the spicy bibimbap recipes.

SWEET WHITE WINES

Sweet wines with a noticeable amount of residual sugar can help tame the heat in spicy dishes, such as for spicy ramen and bibimbap. Consider a German or New York State Riesling, or a California Viognier.

CRISP, DRY, SLIGHTLY ACIDIC, AND EFFERVESCENT WHITE WINES

The light effervescence of a Vinho Verde or Grüner Veltliner is a refreshing contrast to spicy bowls. In the same way, sparkling white wines and rosés are good options. They also pair well with richer bowls, such as the laksa on page 60 and Autumn Ramen on page 52 .

COLD SAKE AND SOJU

A very cold, semidry or semisweet sake—I like the ones that come out of short cans—is delicious and refreshing, and an obvious pairing option with ramen. The popular Korean beverage soju—which is the world's most top-selling alcohol—is classic with the bibimbaps. It's distilled from rice, barley, or potato and is a little sweeter than, but similar to, vodka.

very simple pho

Pho is really all about the broth—and this is especially true of vegetarian pho. When it's an exquisite broth, the noodles and herbs are enough to complete the bowl. This recipe is the simplest possible and makes a light meal. Crispy-fried shallots lend a trace of savoriness, and for juicy crunch, I like to add sprouts or shoots, like mung bean sprouts or sunflower shoots. Use this as a starting point as you experiment with whatever herbs and vegetables you have on hand, drawing from the different treatments in the recipes that follow. Add any vegetables you like such as wilted greens or little wisps of crunchy carrots or radish. Fresh chives, shiso, and lemon verbena used sparingly are lovely additions here. SERVES 4

1½ quarts Vegetarian Pho Broth (page 216) or Shortcut Pho Broth (page 217)

1½ teaspoons sugar

1 teaspoon fine sea salt

8 ounces medium-width rice noodles

2 cups loosely packed fresh basil, mint, and/or cilantro, for garnish

Lime wedges, for garnish

Hot fresh chilies, sliced into very thin rounds, for garnish

Pounded Ginger Pulp (page 247) or freshly grated ginger, for garnish

Chili Oil (page 237), Chili-Garlic Sambal (page 241), store-bought chili-garlic sauce, or another sauce such as sriracha, for garnish

1 cup cubed soft tofu

1 cup crunchy sprouts or shoots, such as mung bean sprouts or sunflower shoots

1 cup Frizzled Shallots (page 244)

• Place the pho broth in a pot and heat to a simmer. Stir in the sugar and salt, then taste, adjusting the seasonings as necessary. Keep covered over low heat until ready to serve.

• Meanwhile, bring a saucepan of water to boil and salt it generously. Add the noodles in a strainer basket or the strainer insert that comes with your stockpot if you have one, and cook until tender, usually 4 to 7 minutes or according to the package instructions. Lift out the noodles, reserving the cooking water, and thoroughly rinse the noodles under cold running water in order to remove excess starch. Quickly dunk them back into the hot water to reheat. Divide the noodles among four bowls.

• Arrange the fresh herbs, lime wedges, chilies, ginger, and chili oil on a large platter or on individual plates at the table.

• Ladle the hot broth over the noodles in each bowl, then divide the tofu, sprouts, and shallots over the top. Serve immediately, allowing diners to add the fresh herbs and the remaining garnishes as they please.

spring pho

Bursting with different shades of tender green things, this bowl is a welcome sight in spring, utilizing some of the season's early arrivals. If you can't find baby bok choy, use baby gem lettuces instead, which show up around the same time (mature bok choy would have an entirely different effect here); baby lettuces, however, don't need to be precooked. Caramelizing the spring onions and scallions adds a rich flavor and texture component to the bowl, similar to a seasoned oil—sweet but deep and silky. Use additional scallions if you're unable to get spring onions. SERVES 4

6 cups Vegetarian Pho Broth (page 216) or Shortcut Pho Broth (page 217)

1½ teaspoons sugar

1 teaspoon fine sea salt

1 bunch spring onions (about 8 ounces)

1 bunch scallions (about 5 ounces)

5 plump garlic cloves

2 tablespoons neutral-tasting oil

1 tablespoon rice vinegar

4 bunches baby bok choy (8 to 10 ounces total), quartered lengthwise through the root

1 cup peas, either young ones with edible pods or shelled mature ones

8 ounces medium-width rice noodles

1 small green chili (serrano, Thai chili, or jalapeño), sliced into very thin rings

2 cups loosely packed mixed fresh herbs, such as chervil, parsley, mint, cilantro, basil, and/or chives, for serving

Lime wedges, for serving

• Place the pho broth in a pot and heat to a simmer. Stir in the sugar and salt and taste, adjusting the seasonings as necessary. Keep covered, off the heat, then bring back to a bare simmer just before serving.

• Trim the root ends off the spring onions and scallions. Thinly slice both the white and green parts. Slice the garlic into thin slabs.

- Heat the oil in a skillet over medium-low heat. Add the spring onions, scallions, and garlic and cook, stirring frequently, until golden brown and caramelized, 10 to 15 minutes. Reduce the heat if the onions begin to burn, or raise it if they seem to be cooking too slowly. Pour in the vinegar and use a wooden spoon to scrape up any browned bits. Remove from the heat.

- Bring a saucepan of salted water to boil. Add the bok choy and cook until the thickest parts of the stem are tender and can be easily pierced with a paring knife, 2 to 3 minutes. Transfer to a plate with a spider skimmer, reserving the cooking water. Add the peas to the water and blanch for 30 seconds, just until the raw bite is gone. Transfer to a plate with a spider skimmer, again reserving the cooking water.

- Add the noodles to the boiling water, in a strainer basket or the strainer insert that comes with your stockpot if you have one, and cook until tender, usually 4 to 7 minutes or according to the package instructions. Lift out the noodles, reserving the cooking water, and thoroughly rinse the noodles under cold running water in order to remove excess starch. Quickly dunk them back into the hot water to reheat. Divide among four bowls.

- Top the noodles in each bowl with the bok choy, peas, caramelized onion mixture, and chilies. Ladle the hot broth over each serving. Serve immediately, passing the herbs and lime wedges at the table.

smoky summer pho

Cooking an eggplant over the open flame of a gas burner is a revelation, producing a silky, succulent texture and a bold, smoky flavor. It can make a small mess, sure—it helps to line the drip pan under your burner with aluminum foil—but the cooking time is less than 10 minutes. In this simple bowl of pho, the eggplant is cut into long strips that integrate into the noodles, and it fully infuses the broth. At the farmers' market, I often find sweet, baby bell peppers, and I like to julienne those and add them raw to this bowl for crunch. A similarly sweet, ripe bell pepper of any color will work much the same way. SERVES 4

6 cups Vegetarian Pho Broth (page 216) or Shortcut Pho Broth (page 217)

1½ teaspoons sugar

1 teaspoon fine sea salt

2 small, thin eggplants, such as Japanese or Chinese (about 8 ounces total)

8 ounces medium-width rice noodles

1 pint cherry tomatoes, quartered

4 baby bell peppers or 1 medium bell pepper, any color, sliced into thin strips

2 serrano chilies, seeded and finely minced

2 cups loosely packed fresh basil, mint, and/or cilantro leaves, for serving

Chili Oil (page 237), for serving

Pounded Ginger Pulp (page 247), for serving

Lime wedges, for serving

• Place the pho broth in a pot and heat to a simmer. Stir in the sugar and salt and taste, adjusting the seasonings as necessary. Keep covered off the heat, then bring back to a bare simmer just before serving.

• Cook the eggplants over the flame of a gas burner: It works best to set a metal cooling rack—one that can bear a few blemishes—directly on top of the grate, then turn the flame to high and set the eggplants directly in the flame. Use heat-safe tongs to turn them periodically, cooking until blistered all over and limp, 4 to 10 minutes, depending on the size of the eggplants. (Alternatively, preheat a broiler to high. Arrange the eggplants on a foil-lined baking sheet. Place close to the heat source and broil for 15 to 20 minutes, carefully turning with tongs periodically, until blistered all over and limp.) Transfer to a colander to drain as you proceed with the rest of the recipe.

• Bring a saucepan of salted water to boil. Add the noodles in a strainer basket or the strainer insert that comes with your stockpot, if you have one, and cook until tender, usually 4 to 7 minutes, or according to the package instructions. Lift out the noodles and thoroughly rinse under cold running water in order to remove excess starch. Quickly dunk them back into the hot water to reheat. Divide among four bowls.

• Gently peel the skin off the eggplants—it should come off easily, in patches and strips—then tear or cut the flesh into long, thin, noodle-like pieces. Divide the eggplant over the noodles, then top each serving with the tomatoes and bell peppers.

• Ladle the pho broth over the noodles and vegetables in each bowl. Sprinkle each serving with the minced chili and serve immediately, passing the herbs, chili oil, ginger, and lime wedges as accompaniments at the table.

VARIATION If your cherry tomatoes are subpar, you can quickly blister them in a skillet to concentrate their flavor and make them sweeter. Place a skillet over medium-high heat. Add a splash of oil and, once hot, add the tomatoes, spreading them out in a single layer. Cook, shaking the pan periodically, until they blister and start to pop, which will take 2 to 4 minutes. Remove from the heat and set aside until ready to use.

fennel pho

Fennel is used in three ways in this light meal. The bulb is thinly sliced and left to soften in a mixture of salt and sugar, and then lends its savory, slightly pickled flavor to the rice noodles; the fronds and crushed seeds are both used for garnish. But fennel's distinct taste doesn't overwhelm—it functions more as a backdrop. Tender chard and carrots, sweet spicy ginger, and salty frizzled shallots help it blossom, and then the herbs and lime juice give it some of pho's expected flavor notes. It's important to slice the fennel bulb thinly, and a mandoline really is the only tool for the job. Thinly sliced rehydrated shiitake mushroom caps are a good addition here, too, if you have them left over from the pho broth or another recipe. SERVES 4

1 large or 2 small bulbs fennel (8 to 10 ounces total)

½ lime, plus more wedges for serving

1¼ teaspoons fine sea salt

2 teaspoons sugar

1 big bunch Swiss chard (about 12 ounces)

3 medium carrots (about 6 ounces total)

6 cups Vegetarian Pho Broth (page 216) or Shortcut Pho Broth (page 217)

8 ounces medium-width rice noodles

½ cup Frizzled Shallots (page 244)

1¼ teaspoons fennel seeds, crushed

1 small green chili (serrano, Thai chili, or jalapeño), sliced into very thin rings, for serving

Pounded Ginger Pulp (page 247) or freshly grated ginger, for serving

2 cups loosely packed fresh basil, mint, and/or cilantro, for serving

• Pick off and reserve the fronds from the fennel. Trim and discard the stalks. Cut the bulb(s) in half lengthwise, as you would an onion. With a paring knife, cut out the firm core, then use a mandoline to slice the fennel into paper-thin shavings, as thin as possible. Transfer to a colander. Squeeze the juice of the lime half over the fennel and toss with ¼ teaspoon of the salt and ½ teaspoon of the sugar. Let stand for 20 minutes, as you prepare the rest of the meal, then gently squeeze the fennel to extract excess moisture.

• Trim the stems from the Swiss chard, reserving them for another use. Cut or tear the leaves into bite-sized pieces. Peel and trim the carrots, then slice into ¼-inch-thick rounds on the bias.

• Place the pho broth in a pot and heat to a simmer. Stir in the remaining 1½ teaspoons sugar and 1 teaspoon salt, then taste, adjusting the seasonings as necessary. Keep covered over low heat until ready to serve.

• Meanwhile, bring a saucepan of water to boil and salt it generously. Add the chard and cook for 1 to 2 minutes, until wilted. Use a spider skimmer or slotted spoon to transfer to a colander to drain, reserving the cooking water. Add the carrots to the boiling water and cook until just tender, 3 to 5 minutes. Transfer to the colander to cool, again reserving the cooking water.

• Add the noodles to the boiling water, in a strainer basket or the strainer insert that comes with your stockpot, if you have one, and cook until tender, usually 4 to 7 minutes or according to the package instructions. Lift out the noodles, reserving the cooking water, and thoroughly rinse the noodles under cold running water in order to remove excess starch. Quickly dunk them back into the hot water to reheat. Divide among four bowls.

• Divide the chard, carrots, and fennel shavings over the noodles in each bowl, then cover each serving with the hot broth. Top with the reserved fennel fronds, shallots, and fennel seeds (about ¼ teaspoon per bowl). Serve immediately, passing the lime wedges, chilies, ginger, and herbs at the table.

winter pho

SUNCHOKES, RADISHES, KALE

Sunchokes (also known as Jerusalem artichokes, though they have no relation to artichokes—they're a species of sunflower) are one of the few exciting items to show up in a CSA box or at the farmers' market during the cold months on the East Coast. Here the shaved sunchokes are a crunchy, refreshing garnish to pho, and create a light dish that's especially welcome after the rich, heavy foods of the holidays. Blanched kale and raw radishes give a lot of texture to the soup, but the extra richness from the garlic chips and some seasoned oil is crucial. If you don't have chili oil or aren't inclined to make it, use the garlic oil (from making the garlic chips) to drizzle over the bowl. SERVES 4

6 cups Vegetarian Pho Broth (page 216) or Shortcut Pho Broth (page 217)

1½ teaspoons sugar

1 teaspoon fine sea salt

5 to 6 ounces sunchokes (about 4 small to medium ones)

6 radishes

4 ounces kale (half of a medium bunch), stemmed

8 ounces medium-width rice noodles

¼ cup Garlic Chips (page 243)

1 cup loosely packed fresh cilantro leaves and tender stems, for serving

Lime wedges, for serving

Chili Oil (page 237) or the garlic oil from making the Garlic Chips, for serving

• Place the pho broth in a pot and heat to a simmer. Stir in the sugar and salt, then taste, adjusting the seasonings as necessary. Keep covered off the heat, then bring back to a bare simmer just before serving.

• Sunchokes often have a lot of dirt caked into the crevices. Wash them thoroughly under running water, then place in a bowl full of cold water to soak, swishing it a few times, and let stand for a few minutes. Drain and repeat as many times as necessary until the water runs clear.

• Rinse out the bowl and fill it again with cold water. Using a mandoline or a sharp knife and steady hand, slice the sunchokes very thinly, about $1/16$ inch thick. Transfer them to the bowl of water as you go to prevent oxidation. Thinly slice the radishes.

• Meanwhile, bring a saucepan of water to boil and salt it generously. Add the kale and blanch for 1 minute, until just tender. Use a spider skimmer to transfer to a colander to drain, reserving the water. Once the kale is cool enough to handle, coarsely chop it.

• Add the noodles to the boiling water, in a strainer basket or the strainer insert that comes with your stockpot, if you have one, and cook until tender, usually 4 to 7 minutes, or according to the package instructions. Lift out the noodles and thoroughly rinse under cold running water in order to remove excess starch. Quickly dunk them back into the hot water to reheat. Divide among four bowls.

• Drain the sunchokes and scatter them over the noodles in each bowl, along with the kale and radishes. Ladle the hot broth over the noodles and vegetables in each bowl and scatter the garlic chips over each serving. Serve immediately, passing the cilantro, lime wedges, and chili oil as accompaniments at the table.

cold rice noodle salad

This delicate salad, inspired by one from a Vietnamese takeout shop in my neighborhood, is light, simple, slurpy, and crisp, and offers a pleasing contrast of cool herbs and spicy chilies. Serve the toppings over the lettuce and the cooked noodles, then, to eat, grab bits of noodles, vegetables, and lettuce with chopsticks and dip them into the sauce bite by bite. As with pho, use a heavy hand with the fresh herbs, since they bring texture and a cloud of aromas that you don't want to miss out on. For this dish—and for many of the cold noodle dishes in the book—it's important that all the components be cold, but especially the dipping sauce. Preparing it in advance not only guarantees this, but also allows for easier assembly later on. SERVES 4

1 serrano chili, seeded if desired, coarsely chopped

1 plump garlic clove, coarsely chopped

1 tablespoon chopped fresh ginger

3 tablespoons brown sugar

½ cup boiling water

3 tablespoons soy sauce

Zest and juice of 1 lime

8 ounces dried medium-width rice noodles or rice vermicelli

1 firm Kirby cucumber, peeled

1 medium carrot, peeled

8 ounces store-bought smoked or baked tofu

4 cups shredded crisp lettuce, such as butter leaf, Boston, romaine, or iceberg

1 red, orange, or yellow bell pepper, cored and sliced into thin strips

2 scallions, green and white parts, thinly sliced on the bias

1 cup thinly sliced or coarsely chopped fresh mint, basil, and/or cilantro, for garnish

¼ cup coarsely chopped roasted peanuts, for garnish

• Combine the chili, garlic, and ginger in a mortar and pound into a rough paste using a pestle. (Alternatively, mince and mash the mixture using a chef's knife, flattening the mixture out on a cutting board by pressing it with the side of the knife and fanning it over the board, until the mixture resembles a paste.) Combine in a small bowl with the brown sugar and the water. Stir

to dissolve the sugar, then add the soy sauce and lime zest and juice. You should have about ¾ cup sauce. Chill thoroughly in the refrigerator for at least 30 minutes, but ideally for a few hours.

• Bring a saucepan of salted water to a boil. Add the noodles and cook until tender, usually 4 to 7 minutes for the thicker noodles or 2 to 4 minutes for vermicelli; be sure to check the package instructions. Drain and rinse under cold running water in order to remove excess starch and to chill the noodles. Drain thoroughly, and keep in the refrigerator until ready to serve.

• Cut the cucumber in half lengthwise and scoop out the seeds with a spoon. Use a mandoline to cut the cucumber and the carrot into long, thin strands. Alternatively, use a vegetable peeler to cut the vegetables into long, thin slabs, then stack the slabs on top of one another and use a sharp knife to cut into thin, noodle-like strips.

• Cut the tofu into about ¼-inch-thick rectangles, then stack them on top of each other and cut into matchsticks.

• Divide the lettuce among four bowls, then top each serving with the cold noodles. Arrange the cucumber, carrot, bell pepper, tofu, and scallions over the noodles in each bowl, then garnish with the herbs and peanuts. You can pass the dipping sauce and spoon it over the noodles at the table, or divide it among four shallow bowls and use chopsticks to dip individual bites into the sauce as you eat.

basic bibimbap

SEARED TOFU, BABY BOK CHOY, PICKLED VEGETABLES

This bibimbap hits all the major flavor touchstones a vegetarian bibimbap should, with savory sesame and soy, tangy and salty pickled vegetables, and a good serving of juicy and mildly bitter greens in the bok choy. It also features one of my favorite, and one of the easiest, tofu cooking methods. As with the other bibimbap recipes in this book, the optional step of crisping the rice mimics what a *dolsot*—the hot stone bowl in which bibimbap is traditionally served—does, by creating a hot crust. It's a step I often skip, but when I do go to the trouble, the crispy patches of rice are something of a delicacy. You can elaborate on or simplify this dish in any number of ways: Combine just rice, a fried egg, and Gochujang Sauce alone for simple comfort food; use store-bought baked or smoked tofu to speed up the recipe; or substitute vegetables—spinach for the bok choy, for example, or Quick Cucumber Pickles (page 231) in place of or in addition to the pickled carrots and radishes. SERVES 4

1 medium carrot, peeled and sliced into thin rounds

6 radishes, sliced into thin rounds

3 teaspoons sugar

½ teaspoon plus 1 pinch of fine sea salt

1 tablespoon rice vinegar

2 to 3 tablespoons neutral-tasting oil

4 bunches baby bok choy (8 to 10 ounces total), thoroughly cleaned and quartered lengthwise through the stems

Freshly ground black pepper

1 to 2 teaspoons toasted sesame oil

14 ounces firm tofu, drained, sliced into thin rectangles, and pressed (see Pressing Tofu, page 119)

2 tablespoons soy sauce

5 cups cooked white or brown rice or mixed grains (see pages 221, 222, and 223), freshly cooked if skipping the rice-crisping step

4 large soft- or crispy-fried eggs (optional; page 225)

2 tablespoons toasted sesame seeds

Gochujang Sauce (page 242) or sriracha, for serving

• Toss the carrot and radishes with 1 teaspoon of the sugar and ½ teaspoon of the salt, and place in a colander for 20 to 30 minutes as you prepare the rest of the meal. Just before serving, rinse and drain the veggies, blot dry with a clean towel, and toss with the rice vinegar.

• Heat a skillet (a nonstick skillet is useful here, for cooking the tofu later) over medium heat and add 1 tablespoon neutral-tasting oil. Add the bok choy and cook, shaking the pan frequently, until the stalks are tender and lightly golden and the leaves are wilted, 3 to 5 minutes. Transfer to a plate. Season with the remaining pinch of salt and several grinds of black pepper. Wipe the pan clean.

• Return the skillet to the heat and add another 1 tablespoon of the neutral-tasting oil and 1 teaspoon of the sesame oil. Carefully add the tofu, sliding it in gently so that the hot oil doesn't splatter and arranging it in a single layer. Drizzle 1 tablespoon soy sauce over the tofu and sprinkle with the remaining 2 teaspoons sugar. Cook until browned and crisp on the bottom. Carefully flip the tofu, trying not to tear it. Drizzle the remaining 1 tablespoon soy sauce over the second side, and cook until browned and crisp. Transfer to the plate with the bok choy.

• To make crispy-base bibimbap rice (optional): Pour out any remaining liquid from the pan, wipe it clean, and return it to the heat. Add the remaining 1 tablespoon neutral-tasting oil and 1 teaspoon toasted sesame oil. Press the rice into the skillet, making a thick cake. Let cook without disturbing for 4 to 5 minutes, until a golden brown crust forms on the bottom of the rice.

• To serve, divide the rice among four bowls, scooping it out of the skillet with a spatula and breaking it apart so that each bowl gets some of the crispy part. Arrange the tofu, bok choy, and pickled carrots and radishes over the rice in each bowl. Top each serving with a fried egg, if using, followed by the sesame seeds. Serve immediately, passing Gochujang Sauce at the table.

spring bibimbap

KIMCHI, SWISS CHARD, QUICK-PICKLED VEGETABLES

Kimchi can be made and eaten any time of the year, but I really crave it in the spring. In this recipe, the kimchi and assorted quick-pickled vegetables are the dominant flavors, making a bright-tasting, tangy bowl. Pickling chard stems is a great way to use them up—they'll add bits of celery-like crunch, and using rainbow chard means lots of extra color, too. Furthermore, the pickled components and the sautéed chard both keep well, meaning that they can be made in advance or packed up as good leftovers. Let the toppings come to room temperature before serving, so that they don't cool down the bowl drastically when you stir all the ingredients together. SERVES 4

2 bunches Swiss chard (1 to 1½ pounds)

1 big Kirby cucumber or half of a conventional cucumber

1 medium carrot, peeled

6 small radishes

1 tablespoon sugar

¾ teaspoon plus 1 pinch of fine sea salt

2 teaspoons rice vinegar

1 to 2 tablespoons neutral-tasting oil

1 to 2 teaspoons toasted sesame oil

1 tablespoon toasted or black sesame seeds

5 cups cooked white or brown rice, or mixed grains (see pages 221, 222, and 223), freshly cooked if skipping the rice-crisping step

Two 2-inch squares toasted nori

2 cups chopped Napa Cabbage or Bok Choy Kimchi, preferably homemade (see page 227)

1 avocado, peeled and sliced

Gochujang Sauce (page 242) or sriracha, for serving

• Trim the stems from the Swiss chard. Cut or tear the leaves into bite-sized pieces and set aside. Reserve half of stems for another use or discard them. Slice the remaining stems into 2-inch lengths, and then into halves, quarters, or eighths to make uniform matchsticks and transfer them to a medium bowl.

• Slice the cucumber into ½-inch-thick rounds, then stack them up and slice into matchsticks. Slice the carrot into thin (less than ¼-inch) rounds. Slice the radishes into thinnest possible rounds. Add the vegetables to the bowl with the chard stems. Toss with the sugar and ¾ teaspoon of the salt and let stand as you prepare the rest of the meal. Just before serving, rinse and drain the veggies, blot dry with a clean towel, and toss with the rice vinegar.

• Meanwhile, place a skillet over medium heat and add 1 tablespoon neutral-tasting oil. Using tongs, add the Swiss chard leaves in increments, adding more as each batch cooks down. Add a big pinch of salt and cook, stirring frequently with the tongs for 3 to 5 minutes, until wilted and the pan appears mostly dry. Remove from the heat and gather up the greens to one side of the pan with a spatula. Holding the chard in place and gently squeezing, tilt the pan over the sink and pour off any excess liquid. (You can do this in a colander if you're worried about accidently dumping the greens into the sink.) Place the chard in a bowl and stir in 1 teaspoon sesame oil and the sesame seeds. Wipe out the skillet.

• To make crispy-base bibimbap rice (optional): Just before serving, heat the remaining 1 table-spoon neutral-tasting oil and 1 teaspoon sesame oil in a wide skillet over medium heat. Press the rice into the skillet, making a thick cake. Let cook without disturbing for 4 to 5 minutes, until a golden brown crust forms on the bottom of the rice.

• Wave the nori squares over the flame of a gas burner a few times, until the corners curl and they turn crisp, or roast under a broiler, flipping periodically. Slice into thin strips with a chef's knife, or crumble with your fingers.

• To serve, use a spatula to scoop out the rice and divide it among four bowls, ensuring that everyone gets some of the crispy part. Top with the Swiss chard, kimchi, and avocado, then use a slotted spoon to add the pickled vegetables to the bowls. Garnish with the nori and serve immediately, passing the Gochujang Sauce at the table.

spicy tofu bibimbap

This method for cooking tofu—mashing it into crumbles with a fork, pan-frying it until crisp, then drizzling it with a sweet, spicy glaze—makes it irresistible to even the most diehard tofu detractor. With its combination of crispiness and juiciness, it is reminiscent of ground meat, and it becomes so thoroughly saturated with flavor that it seasons the entire bowl of rice or grain on its own. The *gochujang* is spicy, but it gets additional kick from a good dose of ground black pepper; cut back on both if you prefer things milder. I balance out the tofu with a simple assortment of crunchy raw vegetables, crisp lettuce, bean sprouts, and chives. You could also adapt this bibimbap by using all of the ingredients as filling for lettuce cups. SERVES 4

One 14-ounce container firm tofu

¼ cup brown sugar

3 tablespoons soy sauce

2 tablespoons rice vinegar

2 to 3 teaspoons *gochujang* (see page 37) or other chili paste (use more for a spicier marinade)

¼ teaspoon freshly ground black pepper

2 to 3 tablespoons neutral-tasting oil

½ cup mung bean sprouts

Boiling water

1 teaspoon toasted sesame oil (optional)

5 cups cooked white or brown rice or mixed grains (see pages 221, 222, and 223), freshly cooked if skipping the rice-crisping step

4 cups shredded crisp lettuce, such as butter leaf, Boston, romaine, or iceberg

2 scallions, green and white parts, thinly sliced

1 cup grated carrots

½ cup thinly sliced radishes

¼ cup minced fresh chives

1 tablespoon toasted sesame seeds, for garnish

Gochujang Sauce (page 242) or sriracha, for serving

• Drain the tofu and blot it dry with a clean kitchen towel or paper towel, then place it in the center of a cutting board and mash it into coarse crumbles with a fork.

- Whisk together the brown sugar, soy sauce, rice vinegar, *gochujang*, and pepper in a small bowl.

- Heat 2 tablespoons of the neutral-tasting oil in a wide skillet over medium heat. Add the crumbled tofu and cook, stirring frequently, until the tofu is golden brown and crispy and the pan is mostly dry, 10 to 15 minutes. Pour in the soy sauce mixture and cook, stirring periodically, until the tofu has absorbed the marinade and the pan is dry, another 5 to 10 minutes. Transfer to a plate to cool.

- Place the bean sprouts in a heat-safe bowl. Cover with boiling water, then immediately drain and refresh under cold running water. Drain thoroughly.

- To make crispy-base bibimbap rice (optional): Just before serving, heat the remaining 1 tablespoon neutral-tasting oil and the sesame oil in a wide skillet over medium heat. Press the rice into the skillet, making a thick cake. Let cook without disturbing for 4 or 5 minutes, until a golden brown crust forms on the bottom of the rice.

- To serve, use a spatula to scoop out the rice and divide it among four bowls, ensuring that everyone gets some of the crispy part. Top with the tofu, bean sprouts, lettuce, scallions, carrot, radishes, and chives, then garnish each serving with the sesame seeds. Serve immediately, passing the Gochujang Sauce at the table.

roasted vegetable bibimbap

BROCCOLI RABE, BUTTERNUT SQUASH, SHIITAKE

This bowl has a terrific balance of autumnal flavors and a mix of foliage-inspired colors, with its sweet squash, earthy and juicy shiitakes, and slightly bitter broccoli rabe. All the vegetables are oven-roasted, and you can crisp the rice while they're cooking, making this a relatively quick and efficient bowl to throw together. Roasted mushrooms are easy and addictive, adding bulk and chew. As for the squash, cutting it into domino-like slabs creates more surface area for caramelization. You can use any winter squash here, such as kabocha (which doesn't require peeling) or acorn—or even sweet potatoes—just cut them to about the same size, and watch closely during roasting. SERVES 4

1 small or ½ a medium-to-large butternut squash (about 1½ pounds)

1 bunch broccoli rabe

8 ounces shiitake mushrooms

2 to 3 tablespoons neutral-tasting oil

2 tablespoons soy sauce

1 tablespoon brown sugar

2 teaspoons *gochujang* (see page 37) or store-bought *sambal oelek*

1 teaspoon toasted sesame oil (optional)

5 cups cooked white or brown rice or mixed grains (see pages 221, 222, and 223), freshly cooked if skipping the rice-crisping step

4 large soft- or crispy-fried eggs (page 225)

1 cup sprouts or shoots, such as broccoli sprouts, mung bean sprouts, or sunflower shoots, for garnish

½ cup Quick Cucumber Pickles (page 231), for optional garnish

Lime wedges, for garnish

Gochujang Sauce (page 242) or sriracha, for serving

• Preheat the oven to 400°F.

• Trim the ends off of the butternut squash, then cut in half crosswise where the bottom begins to swell. Stand each piece upright on a sturdy cutting board and, with a sharp chef's knife, carefully cut off the skin in strips, slicing down and working all the way around the squash.

(Alternatively, use a vegetable peeler, but be thorough in removing all of the pale white skin.) Slice the bottom part in half lengthwise and scoop out the seeds, then, with the wide, flat side down, slice the squash into strips about ½ inch thick. Cut the top section of squash into ½-inch-thick slabs as well, then stack them on top of each other and cut into thirds or quarters so that they're about the size of dominoes.

• Trim away and discard the tough stems of the broccoli rabe, reserving only the leaves and the flowering parts. Trim the stems off the mushrooms and discard; if large, slice the caps in half.

• Whisk together 2 tablespoons of the neutral-tasting oil, the soy sauce, brown sugar, and *gochujang*. Arrange the prepared squash and mushrooms on one baking sheet, and the broccoli rabe on another. Divide the sauce between the two pans and use your hands to toss the vegetables so that they're evenly coated. Transfer both pans to the oven. Cook the broccoli rabe for 5 to 8 minutes, until collapsed and the thicker parts of the stems are tender. Cook the squash and mushrooms for 15 to 20 minutes, until the squash is caramelized and tender and the mushrooms are juicy and slightly shrunken (the mushrooms are forgiving—ensuring that the squash is cooked all the way through is the priority). Cover the baking sheets with foil to keep them warm until ready to serve.

• To make crispy-base bibimbap rice (optional): Just before serving, heat the remaining 1 tablespoon neutral-tasting oil and the sesame oil in a wide skillet over medium heat. Press the rice into the skillet, making a thick cake. Let cook without disturbing for 4 to 5 minutes, until a golden brown crust forms on the bottom of the rice.

• To serve, use a spatula to scoop out the rice and divide it among four bowls, ensuring that everyone gets some of the crispy part. Top with the squash, broccoli rabe, and mushrooms— including any marinade left on the baking sheets—and place 1 fried egg on top of the vegetables in each bowl. Garnish with the sprouts or shoots, pickles, if using, and lime wedges, and serve immediately, passing the Gochujang Sauce at the table.

winter bibimbap

Here's another good way to incorporate *gochujang*, the Korean fermented chili paste, into weeknight cooking. It's used to flavor the oil the sweet potatoes are tossed in before roasting, turning them spicy-sweet, crispy-edged, and good enough to be served alone as a side dish, and making them the highlight here. "Massaging" kale is a method of softening and seasoning it by rubbing salt into the shredded leaves. I don't always remove the kale ribs, but in this bowl, I recommend it, as that added crunch is a little unpleasant here (if you want to use the stems and ribs, julienne them finely along with the leaves, as described on page 145). And massaging, rather than sautéing or boiling, has the added perk of eliminating a skillet from the stove. SERVES 4

1 to 2 tablespoons plus 2 teaspoons neutral-tasting oil

1½ teaspoons *gochujang* (see page 37)

1 teaspoon minced garlic

1 to 2 teaspoons toasted sesame oil

1 pound sweet potatoes (2 medium or 1 large), peeled if desired and cut into ¾-inch dice

1 large bunch kale (about 12 ounces), stemmed

½ teaspoon fine sea salt

2 teaspoons rice vinegar

1 cup mung bean sprouts, rinsed

Boiling water

5 cups cooked white or brown rice or mixed grains (see pages 221, 222, and 223), freshly cooked if skipping the rice-crisping step

4 large soft- or crispy-fried eggs (page 225)

2 tablespoons toasted sesame seeds, for garnish

Gochujang Sauce (page 242) or sriracha, for serving

• Preheat the oven to 400°F.

• In a medium bowl, whisk together 1 tablespoon of the neutral-tasting oil, the *gochujang*, garlic, and 1 teaspoon of the sesame oil. Add the diced sweet potatoes and stir to thoroughly coat, then spread out on a baking sheet in an even layer. Roast for 12 to 16 minutes, until tender.

• Meanwhile, shred the kale: Roll stacks of leaves into cigar shapes, then cut into thin strips. Add to a mixing bowl with the salt and gently "massage" with your hands until the kale is glistening and collapsed. Give the greens a squeeze, and pour off any liquid that collects in the bottom of the bowl. Stir in 2 teaspoons of the neutral-tasting oil and the rice vinegar.

• Place the bean sprouts in a heat-safe bowl and cover with boiling water. Immediately drain in a sieve and rinse thoroughly under cold running water, then drain again thoroughly.

• To make crispy-base bibimbap rice (optional): Just before serving, heat the remaining 1 tablespoon neutral-tasting oil and 1 teaspoon sesame oil in a wide skillet over medium heat. Press the rice into the skillet, making a thick cake. Let cook without disturbing for 4 to 5 minutes, until a golden brown crust forms on the bottom of the rice.

• To serve, use a spatula to scoop out the rice and divide it among four bowls, ensuring that everyone gets some of the crispy part. Divide the sweet potatoes, kale, and bean sprouts among the bowls. Top each bowl with 1 fried egg. Garnish with the sesame seeds and serve immediately, passing the Gochujang Sauce at the table.

kimchi fried rice bowl

Kimchi fried rice is right at home in the canon of comfort foods and can be put together quickly. The ideal for all fried rice is to achieve individual grains that are slightly crisp, caramelized, and saturated with flavor. To avoid gloppy, slippery rice, rule number one is to not overfill the skillet, which is why this recipe yields only two servings. Rule number two is to make sure the pan is hot when you add the rice. I also find that a nonstick skillet is terrific for fried rice, requiring less oil than a standard skillet and creating much less of a mess to clean afterward. Stir-fried lettuce has a wonderful, succulent texture and mild flavor that complements the bold kimchi flavors here. Hydroponic lettuces are a great option because of their crispy texture. SERVES 2

1 tablespoon neutral-tasting oil

1 teaspoon toasted sesame oil, plus more for drizzling

1 small onion, cut into thin strips

2/3 cup Napa Cabbage or Bok Choy Kimchi, preferably homemade (see page 227), drained and coarsely chopped

2 1/2 cups day-old white or brown rice or mixed grains (see pages 221, 222, and 223)

1/2 teaspoon fine sea salt

1/2 teaspoon sugar

1 tablespoon kimchi brine

3 teaspoons soy sauce

1/2 cup coarsely chopped fresh cilantro leaves and tender stems, or 2 tablespoons minced fresh chives

2 scallions, white and green parts, thinly sliced

1 teaspoon rice vinegar

4 cups shredded crisp lettuce, such as butter lettuce, Boston, romaine, or iceberg, thoroughly dried

2 large soft-fried eggs (page 225)

1/4 cup Quick Cucumber Pickles (optional; page 231)

1 teaspoon toasted sesame seeds, for garnish

• Heat the neutral-tasting oil and 1 teaspoon sesame oil in a nonstick skillet over medium heat. Add the onion and cook, stirring periodically, until soft and translucent, 5 to 7 minutes. Add the kimchi and cook for 2 to 3 minutes more, until fragrant and the kimchi begins to brown in parts. Raise the heat slightly, then add the rice, crumbling it into the pan with your hands or using a spatula to break it up. Sprinkle ¼ teaspoon of the salt and ¼ teaspoon of the sugar over the rice and cook, stirring frequently, for 4 to 5 minutes, until the pan is dry.

• Clear a small space in the middle of the skillet and pour in the kimchi brine and 2 teaspoons soy sauce. Let the liquid bubble for about 10 seconds, which encourages caramelization of the soy sauce, then stir it into the rice. Cook for 3 to 5 minutes more, until the pan is dry again. Quickly stir in the cilantro and scallions, reserving a little of each for garnish, then divide the rice mixture between two bowls and cover with foil to keep warm.

• Return the skillet to the heat. Add the remaining 1 teaspoon soy sauce and the rice vinegar, allowing it to bubble and caramelize, then add the lettuce. Sprinkle with the remaining ¼ teaspoon salt and ¼ teaspoon sugar and cook, stirring constantly, for just 30 to 45 seconds, until the lettuce is half wilted—it should still have a bit of crunch. Divide the lettuce over the fried rice in each bowl. Top each bowl with 1 fried egg, the pickles, if using, and any reserved herbs and scallions, and garnish with the sesame seeds.

sushi bowl

This sushi roll deconstructed into a bowl works wonderfully because it's such a logical way to simplify sushi for serving at home. My favorite vegetarian sushi has lots of contrasting flavors and textures, and this bowl centers on tender rounds of honey-soy glazed sweet potato, which offer contrast to the creamy avocado, crisp cucumber, and bitter daikon radish—all common sushi roll components—arranged on top of a pile of sticky sushi rice. If pressed for time, skip the glazing step—but you may just need a little bit more soy sauce to season the bowl at the table. And just as with a sushi roll, I like to stir the wasabi into my dish of soy sauce at the table, until it's spicy enough to give me an adrenaline rush. SERVES 4

1 medium sweet potato, peeled if desired (10 to 12 ounces)

2 tablespoons honey

1 tablespoon soy sauce, plus more for serving

1 tablespoon neutral-tasting oil

One 4-inch length daikon radish

1 small cucumber

1 avocado

Four 2-inch squares toasted nori

1 tablespoon rice or brown rice vinegar

½ teaspoon fine sea salt

¼ teaspoon sugar

5 cups freshly cooked short-grain white or brown rice (see pages 221 and 222)

2 tablespoons toasted sesame seeds

2 scallions, white and green parts, thinly sliced on the bias, for garnish

Wasabi paste, for serving

Pickled Ginger (page 117), for serving

• Slice the sweet potato into rounds about ¾ inch thick. Fill a saucepan fitted with a steamer unit with about ½ inch of water and bring to a simmer. Add the sweet potato to the steamer basket, cover, and cook until just tender, 7 to 10 minutes. Transfer to a plate or bowl to cool until safe to handle.

• In a small bowl, whisk together the honey and soy sauce. Heat a skillet over medium-high heat. Add the oil and, when it shimmers, arrange the potato in a single layer in the pan. Cook for 1 to 2 minutes, until it just begins to color and get crisp. Flip and repeat on the other side. Pour in the honey-soy mixture and cook until the sauce thickens and the potato is glazed, turning it frequently to ensure that it's well coated, 1 to 2 minutes more. Remove from the heat.

• Peel the daikon and cut it into matchsticks about ¼ inch thick and 2 inches long. Do the same with the cucumber. Peel the avocado and slice it into thin slabs.

• Just before serving, wave the nori squares over the flame of a gas burner a few times until the corners curl and they turn crisp, or roast under a broiler, flipping periodically. Slice into thin strips with a chef's knife, or crumble with your fingers.

• Stir the rice vinegar, salt, and sugar together until the solids dissolve. Drizzle over the hot cooked rice, add the sesame seeds, and stir gently to combine. Taste and add a few more sprinkles of vinegar if desired.

• Divide the rice among four bowls. Arrange the glazed potato slices, daikon, cucumber, and avocado on top of the rice in each bowl. Sprinkle the nori over the top of each serving and garnish with the scallions. Serve with individual dishes for the additional soy sauce, the wasabi, and pickled ginger at the table.

pickled ginger

Pickled ginger is easy enough to find at grocery stores and Asian markets, but it's also quite easy to make at home once it's all peeled and sliced. There's nothing wrong with thick pieces of ginger that still have a little crunch, but the thinner you slice it—a mandoline comes in very handy —the more similar it'll be to what's found at sushi restaurants. MAKES ABOUT ½ CUP

4 ounces small, firm fresh ginger, peeled

½ cup white vinegar or unseasoned rice vinegar

¼ cup sugar

¾ teaspoon salt

• Using a mandoline, or a sharp knife and steady hand, slice the ginger into the thinnest possible pieces. I like to slice it the bias, rather than into rounds, because it creates longer pieces.

• Place the ginger in a saucepan and cover with cold water. Bring to a boil and cook for 5 minutes. Drain and refresh under cold running water. Cover again with water, boil for 5 minutes, drain, and refresh. Taste the ginger—it should be tender and have very little raw bite left. If it still seems raw, repeat this boil-drain-refresh step once more. Drain thoroughly, then pack into a heat-safe jar or container.

• Combine the vinegar, sugar, and salt in a small saucepan and bring to a boil. Reduce the heat and simmer, stirring, until the solids dissolve, 1 to 2 minutes. Pour over the ginger and let stand until completely cool then cover with an airtight lid. Stored this way in the refrigerator, it will keep for several weeks.

ginger-scallion rice bowl

GRILLED TOFU, MARINATED CUCUMBERS, CRISP LETTUCE

The preparation of my ginger-scallion sauce is streamlined by throwing every-thing into a food processor. The sauce doubles as both a marinade for the grilled tofu and a condiment for the finished bowl, allowing for that distinctive sweet and spicy flavor to penetrate everything. (If you have any left over, don't waste it! It's delicious on soba noodles.) I pair the tofu with a simple cucumber salad and shredded lettuce, which creates texture contrast and lots of fresh juiciness. The leftovers, packed separately, keep terrifically well. SERVES 4

1 bunch scallions (8 to 10 ounces), white and green parts trimmed, cleaned, and sliced roughly into 1- to 2-inch pieces

2 heaping tablespoons coarsely minced fresh ginger

2 tablespoons plus 1½ teaspoons rice vinegar

3 garlic cloves, coarsely chopped

1 tablespoon sugar

1 tablespoon soy sauce

¾ teaspoon fine sea salt

½ teaspoon freshly ground black pepper

Scant ¼ teaspoon red pepper flakes

5 tablespoons neutral-tasting oil

One 14-ounce container firm tofu, sliced and pressed dry (opposite)

2 Kirby cucumbers

½ teaspoon toasted sesame oil

2 teaspoons toasted sesame seeds

5 cups freshly cooked white or brown rice or mixed grains (see pages 221, 222, and 223)

2 cups shredded crisp lettuce, such as butter leaf, Boston, romaine, or iceberg

¼ cup Frizzled Shallots (page 244), for garnish

• Combine the scallions, ginger, 2 tablespoons of the vinegar, the garlic, sugar, soy sauce, ½ teaspoon of the salt, the black pepper, and red pepper flakes in a food processor. Pulse until a coarse paste forms. Add the neutral-tasting oil and pulse a few times more. Taste and adjust the seasoning as necessary.

• Arrange the tofu in a rectangular pan or a resealable bag. Add half of the ginger-scallion sauce to the tofu, gently flipping the tofu to ensure that it's thoroughly coated. Let stand for at least 30 minutes, or for several hours, covered with plastic wrap if in a pan, in the refrigerator. Reserve the remaining sauce.

• Peel the cucumbers, if desired, and slice in half lengthwise. Scoop out the seeds with a spoon, then slice on the bias into wedges about ¼ inch thick. Combine with the remaining 1½ teaspoons vinegar and ¼ teaspoon salt, the toasted sesame oil, and sesame seeds in a small bowl.

• Heat one side of a grill to a medium-high flame and grease the grates.

• Arrange the marinated tofu on the grill. Cook without disturbing for 4 to 6 minutes, so that grill marks show, then carefully flip to cook the other side. Transfer to a plate.

• To serve, divide the rice among four bowls. Top each serving with the grilled tofu and the cucumbers. Add a pile of the lettuce and 1 heaping tablespoon of the reserved ginger-scallion sauce to each bowl, then garnish with the frizzled shallots.

pressing tofu

Pressing tofu firms up its texture by extracting water. For many tofu treatments, that water is then replaced with a flavorful marinade.

You can press the whole block or slice it into rectangles or squares first. For most purposes, I slice it into thin rectangles (creating lots of surface area for crisping and caramelizing). Make sure that they're of even thickness.

Lay out a clean kitchen towel on a cutting board. Arrange the tofu block or slices in the center of one half of the towel, then fold the rest of the towel over. Place a baking sheet or a 9-by-13-inch pan on top of the tofu, then weigh this down with one or two heavy items—a cast-iron skillet works, or a few cans of beans or tomatoes.

The tofu can be pressed for anywhere from 20 minutes to many hours. The longer it's pressed, the drier and more pliable its texture becomes.

grain bowls

Years ago I ate at one of America's most famous vegan restaurants, Café Gratitude, in Los Angeles. All of the menu items there are affirmations—"I am Bountiful," "I am Fortified," "I am Whole." This can seem a little awkward if you aren't prepared, but I found the dishes were irresistible: healthy, hearty, well crafted, full of bold flavors and textures, and complete. All the components harmonized beautifully, making each one more than the sum of its parts. These were bowls to aspire to.

Like them, the meals in this chapter are both substantial and informal—component cooking at its best. Into the bottom of each bowl goes a grain and maybe some tender greens; on top, a scattering of fresh, pickled, or cooked vegetables and some proteins, nuts, or seeds. A few fresh herbs or frizzled shallots may be used as garnish; there might be a poached egg on top too; then all the gaps are filled with some kind of delicious sauce, such as a lemony tahini, a cilantro-based green sauce, or a pulpy ginger and lime juice drizzle. The idea is to lay out everything necessary for a meal—grain or starch, vegetables, proteins, sauce, garnishes—and, as long as the flavor profiles align and the textures are complementary, to combine them in a bowl.

Many of these recipes reflect the way I cook for myself on those nights when cooking feels like a chore. Nothing in particular sounds appetizing and the fridge and cupboards are "bare." But wait—I *do* have some lentils and some quinoa. And there's that half of an onion, and what am I going to do with that smidge of leftover yogurt and the handful of lettuce? Well, maybe I could make *mujadara*, a Middle Eastern dish of lentils and rice, but swap out the rice for quinoa? Similarly, a few stubs of eggplant and zucchini and my short patience prompted the shortcut ratatouille that's the basis for the Ratatouille Polenta Bowl. Just about any meal can be served in a bowl, as the recipes in this chapter suggest.

breakfast rice bowl

MAPLE-GLAZED SWEET POTATOES, SPINACH, FRIED EGGS

This bowl is perfect as a lazy breakfast or brunch for two. It takes its cues from the weekend spread typical of the American table—hash browns, pancakes, fried eggs—but with a lot more color. Glazing sweet potatoes with maple syrup practically makes them candy, and the added step of "frying" the day-old rice in the dregs of syrup soaks up all the good flavors from the pan. I like to drizzle the fried eggs with a splash of soy sauce during the last minute or so, and a dollop of an extra-tangy yogurt keeps the spice and sweetness in check. Pass hot sauce—in this case, *sambal* or another one you like—at the table. And as with Kimchi Fried Rice (page 111), you don't want to crowd the pan when making fried rice, which is why this recipe serves only two. SERVES 2

5 ounces spinach

4 tablespoons neutral-tasting oil

2 pinches of fine sea salt

1 small or ½ large onion, sliced into thin strips or rings

1 small sweet potato, peeled if desired (5 to 6 ounces)

⅛ teaspoon cayenne pepper

1 tablespoon good-quality maple syrup

3 cups day-old cooked white or brown rice or mixed grains (see pages 221, 222, and 223)

2 large crisp-fried eggs (page 225)

2 tablespoons good-quality plain yogurt

Freshly ground black pepper

Chili-Garlic Sambal (page 241) or store-bought chili-garlic paste or hot sauce, for serving

• If using mature spinach, trim off any tough stems.

• Heat 1 tablespoon of the oil in a medium skillet over medium heat. Add the spinach and 1 pinch of salt and cook, turning the spinach with tongs, until wilted but still bright green, 1 to 2 minutes. Gather the greens to one side of the pan and, holding the pan over the sink, press against the greens with a spatula and pour off the excess liquid. (You can do this in a colander if you're worried about accidentally dumping the greens into the sink.) Transfer the greens to a plate or bowl, wipe out the skillet, and return it to the heat.

• Raise the heat slightly and add the remaining 3 tablespoons of the oil to the skillet. Once hot, add the onion. Cook, stirring frequently, for 8 to 15 minutes, until reddish-golden brown and beginning to crisp. Use a slotted spoon to transfer the onions to a paper towel–lined plate to drain, leaving the oil in the skillet. Pour off all but about 1½ tablespoons of the oil, and return the skillet to the heat.

• Slice the sweet potato in half lengthwise and then into quarters. Slice each quarter into ¼-inch-thick pieces.

• Add the cayenne to the hot oil, followed by the sweet potato. Sprinkle with another big pinch of salt and spread the sweet potato into as even a layer as space allows. Cook for 2 to 3 minutes without disturbing, until it takes on some color. Flip and repeat. Continue cooking until the sweet potato is light golden brown and tender, 4 to 7 minutes total (check by piercing with a paring knife). Drizzle the maple syrup over the sweet potato and toss to coat. Cook for another 1 to 2 minutes, until the maple syrup thickens and caramelizes, glazing the sweet potatoes. Use a slotted spoon to transfer the sweet potato to the plate with the spinach, leaving the maple syrup and oil in the skillet. Return the skillet to the heat.

• Add the rice to the skillet, breaking it up with a spatula. Cook for 3 to 5 minutes, stirring constantly, until the rice is heated through and the pan appears dry.

• Divide the hot rice between two bowls, then divide the spinach and potato over the rice. Top each serving with 1 fried egg and garnish with the fried onions. Dollop with 1 tablespoon of the yogurt, top with a few grinds of black pepper, and serve, passing hot sauce at the table.

savory oatmeal bowl

SAUTÉED GREENS, POACHED EGGS, TOGARASHI

Savory oatmeal makes a terrific weekend brunch on return from the farmers' market (and it's just as good for lunch or dinner). One way to get extra-creamy oatmeal is to cook the oats in a combination of milk and water. I sometimes use regular milk, but this dish is good with soy milk, too. (For soy milk, examine the ingredients and pick one that contains only soybeans—preferably organic, whole ones—and water; no preservatives, emulsifiers, sweeteners, or other additives. Westsoy is the brand I like best.) That said, it's absolutely fine to cook the oats in just water. SERVES 4

1 tablespoon plus 1 teaspoon neutral-tasting oil

1 cup steel cut oats

2½ cups water

1 cup good-quality soy milk

½ teaspoon fine sea salt

¼ cup minced fresh chives

1 bunch spinach or Swiss chard (about 12 ounces)

2 large garlic cloves, thinly sliced

1 teaspoon freshly grated ginger

4 large poached eggs (page 226)

3 scallions, white and green parts, thinly sliced

4 teaspoons soy sauce

Chili Oil (page 237), Chili-Bean Oil (page 240), or toasted sesame oil, for serving

Togarashi Blend, homemade or store-bought (page 245), for serving

• Place a medium saucepan over medium-high heat and add 1 teaspoon of the oil. Once hot, add the oats. Cook, stirring frequently, until they darken a shade and are fragrant, 3 to 5 minutes. Pour in the water and soy milk. As soon as the mixture comes to a boil, reduce the heat to low, stir in the salt, partially cover the pan, and cook for 18 to 22 minutes, until the oats reach the desired thickness. Stir in the chives. Let stand, covered, until ready to assemble. (If the oatmeal thickens too much as it sits, stir in a few tablespoons of water to loosen it.)

• If using mature spinach, pick off any long, tough stems. If using chard, trim off the stems, reserve them for another use, and cut the leaves into bite-sized pieces.

• Meanwhile, heat a skillet over medium-low heat and add the remaining 1 tablespoon oil. Once hot, add the garlic and ginger. Stir for a moment, then add the greens. If the greens are dry, add about 2 teaspoons water to the pan. Cook until just wilted. Gather the greens in one corner of the pan with a spatula and, tilting the pan over the sink, press on the greens to extract and pour off as much liquid as possible. (You can do this in a colander if you're worried about accidentally dumping the greens into the sink.) Transfer the greens to a plate or cutting board.

• Divide the oatmeal among four bowls. Top with the greens and 1 egg each per bowl, then top each serving with the scallions and 1 teaspoon each of soy sauce. Serve immediately, passing the flavored oil and togarashi at the table. Garnish liberally with the togarashi.

NOTE Leftover oatmeal keeps for several days stored in an airtight container in the refrigerator. Reheat on the stove, stirring in a few tablespoons of water, milk, or soy milk until it reaches your desired consistency (it thickens considerably as it cools).

green sauce bowl à la laurie colwin

WATERCRESS SAUCE, STEAMED VEGETABLES, QUICK-PICKLED RADISHES

The late Laurie Colwin's *Home Cooking* and *More Home Cooking* are two of my favorite food books. I belong to a dinner club that was founded in Colwin's honor, and have cooked most of the recipes in her books but what I love most are her inviting voice, funny quirks, and great writing. The sauce in this recipe was inspired by Jeannete Kossuth's Green Sauce from an essay in *Home Cooking* on how to satisfy fussy eaters—vegetarians, vegans, and fad dieters—by serving them steamed vegetables with the sauce. I've changed Colwin's recipe a little by using less oil and bulking it up into a more substantial meal. I add any extra herbs or even tender lettuce—cilantro, parsley, basil, romaine, arugula, even radish greens if they look vibrant and perky—into the blender with the watercress. Feel free to play around with the toppings, too. SERVES 4

6 medium radishes

½ teaspoon fine sea salt

½ teaspoon sugar

3 tablespoons apple cider vinegar or sherry vinegar

1 tablespoon water

1 bunch watercress (about 4 ounces), cleaned and dried

4 scallions

½ cup loosely packed mixed fresh herbs or peppery greens, such as parsley, cilantro, basil, arugula or radish greens

⅓ to ½ cup mild-flavored olive oil

1 heaping tablespoon Dijon mustard

1 large garlic clove

½ teaspoon salt

1 small head broccoli (8 to 10 ounces)

1½ cups small, waxy potatoes (8 to 10 ounces), scrubbed clean

1 medium zucchini or other summer squash (8 ounces)

5 cups freshly cooked mixed grains (see page 223)

½ cup toasted walnuts or cashews, for garnish

2 tablespoons capers, rinsed and coarsely chopped, for garnish

• Use a mandoline or a chef's knife to cut the radishes into thin rounds. Toss in a bowl with the sea salt and sugar and let stand for 15 to 20 minutes. Gather the radishes into your hands and gently squeeze out and pour off the liquid. Cover the radishes with the vinegar and the water. Let stand as you prepare the rest of the meal.

• Pick off about 2 cups of watercress leaves and sprigs and set them aside to use later as garnish. Thinly slice the white parts of the scallions and set them aside. Cut the pale and dark green parts into 1- to 2-inch segments.

• Put ⅓ cup oil and the mustard in a blender, followed by the remaining watercress stems and leaves, the green parts of the scallions, the herbs, the garlic, and salt. Puree until very smooth, pouring in additional olive oil by the tablespoon as needed to loosen up the sauce. Process until smooth.

• Prepare the vegetables: Trim the broccoli florets off the stalk and cut the florets into bite-sized pieces. Use a vegetable peeler to remove the outer layer of skin from the stalk, then cut the stalk into bite-sized pieces. Cut the potatoes in halves or quarters. Trim the ends off the zucchini and then cut it into ½-inch-thick rounds.

• Steam the vegetables: Fill a saucepan with about ½ inch of water and bring to a simmer. Insert a steamer basket and add the broccoli. Cover the pot and cook for 4 to 6 minutes, until the broccoli is easily pierced with a paring knife. Use tongs to remove the broccoli from the basket and transfer to a plate to cool, reserving the steaming water. Add the potatoes to the steamer basket. Cover and cook for 5 to 7 minutes, until tender and easily pierced with a paring knife. Use tongs to move the potatoes to the plate with the broccoli and add the zucchini to the steamer basket. Cook for 3 or 4 minutes, until tender, then add to the plate with the other vegetables. (Alternatively, use a metal or bamboo stacking steamer unit to steam all the vegetables at once, in separate layers.)

• To serve, divide the cooked grains among four bowls and divide the steamed vegetables on top. Add dollops of the green sauce to each bowl—about 2 generous tablespoons per bowl to start. Garnish each serving with the nuts, capers, a little pile of radishes, the reserved scallion whites, and the reserved watercress leaves. Serve immediately, passing additional green sauce at the table.

ratatouille polenta bowl

In most ratatouille recipes, mushiness is the fatal flaw. Salting the eggplant and zucchini draws out their excess water, seasons them, and ensures that they crisp rather than steam when they hit the hot pan. The cubed vegetables are carefully pan-fried in separate batches, to ensure perfection. Be patient and attentive; it'll be worth it. Instead of a slow-cooked tomato sauce as a binder, cherry tomatoes are cooked quickly over high heat until they burst, resulting in bright tomato flavor and a chunky consistency that functions more as a component than as a saucy backdrop. Serving this ratatouille with a poached egg and over soft polenta is my favorite, but it can also be served with rice, mixed grains, or farro. SERVES 4

2 medium Japanese eggplants or ½ large globe eggplant (8 to 10 ounces)

1½ teaspoons fine sea salt

2 medium zucchini (about 1 pound)

5 tablespoons olive oil

1 pint ripe cherry tomatoes, halved

2 teaspoons minced garlic

2 teaspoons minced fresh oregano

Freshly ground black pepper

4 cups water

1 cup polenta (not instant)

4 large soft- or crispy-fried eggs (page 225) or poached eggs (page 226), optional

¼ cup crumbled semi-firm goat cheese

1 cup loosely packed fresh basil leaves

• If desired, peel the eggplant with a vegetable peeler. Dice into ½-inch cubes. Toss with ½ teaspoon of the salt and transfer to a colander or spread out on a paper towel–lined baking sheet. Let stand for 20 to 30 minutes. Blot dry with a clean kitchen towel.

• Trim the ends off the zucchini and dice into ½-inch cubes. Toss with another ½ teaspoon salt and transfer to a separate colander or paper towel–lined baking sheet. Let stand for 20 to 30 minutes. Blot dry with a clean kitchen towel.

• Heat 1 tablespoon of the oil in your widest skillet or Dutch oven over medium-high heat. Add the tomatoes, spreading in a single layer. Cook for 4 to 7 minutes, until they blister, swirling the pan periodically. (Be cautious of oil splattering.) Add the garlic, stir until fragrant, then transfer the tomato mixture to a mixing bowl.

• Wipe out the skillet and return it to the heat. Add 2 tablespoons of the oil. Add the eggplant. If it doesn't fit in a comfortable single layer, cook it in two batches. Cook for 5 to 7 minutes, turning periodically, until golden brown all over on the outside and tender on the inside but not mushy—check for doneness by tasting frequently. Adjust the heat as needed, raising it if the eggplant doesn't seem be browning quickly enough or lowering it if it starts to burn. Transfer to the bowl with the tomatoes.

• Return the skillet to the heat and add the remaining 2 tablespoons oil. Add the zucchini, again cooking in two batches if it doesn't fit in a comfortable single layer. Cook for 3 to 5 minutes, turning periodically, until golden brown all over and crisp-tender on the inside. Adjust the heat as needed. Transfer to the bowl with the tomatoes and eggplant. Sprinkle the oregano over the vegetables, grind a few turns of black pepper over, and stir gently to combine.

• While the vegetables are cooking, prepare the polenta. Bring the water to boil in a saucepan. Add the remaining ½ teaspoon salt and sprinkle in the polenta while whisking constantly. When the water comes back to a boil, reduce the heat to a gentle, gurgling simmer. Continue whisking until the grains begin to suspend in the liquid rather than sink to the bottom, and then stir periodically until the polenta is thick and grains are tender, usually 15 to 25 minutes, but check the package instructions and taste as you go. Keep covered until ready to serve. If it thickens too much as it sits, you can thin it with a bit of hot water just before serving.

• Divide the polenta among four bowls, then spoon the ratatouille over the polenta in each. Top each serving with 1 egg, if using, then the goat cheese. Tear the basil leaves over the top and serve immediately.

grilled vegetable couscous bowl

GRILLED EGGPLANT AND CORN, POUNDED GINGER DRIZZLE

All the summery goodness—eggplant and tofu cross-hatched with grill marks, corn, tomatoes, mint, and a pulpy ginger topping—harmonizes beautifully in this bowl, bursting with juicy flavors. I especially like couscous here because it's so quick-cooking and only requires covering with boiling water. As with quinoa and some of the other grains in this book, a quick toast of the grains deepens its flavor. I prefer to cut the grilled corn off the cob for serving, but you can also chop each cob in half and place two pieces in each bowl. SERVES 4

1 tablespoon soy sauce

1 tablespoon brown sugar

2 teaspoons toasted sesame oil

One 14-ounce container firm tofu, sliced and pressed (see page 119)

2 Japanese eggplants (8 to 10 ounces), or equivalent weight other small eggplants

3 teaspoons fine sea salt

1/2 ounce fresh ginger (1 thumb-sized piece), peeled

2 scallions, white and green parts, thinly sliced

1 tablespoon toasted sesame seeds

1/2 teaspoon sugar

2 teaspoons lime juice, from about 1/2 lime

2 tablespoons neutral-tasting oil, plus more for brushing

1 1/2 cups couscous

3 cups boiling water

4 ears corn, husked

1 large ripe tomato (about 12 ounces), cored and diced, or 1 cup cherry tomatoes, halved if large

1/4 cup loosely packed fresh basil or mint leaves, for garnish

• Whisk together the soy sauce, brown sugar, and sesame oil for the marinade. Arrange the pressed tofu in a shallow dish, then drizzle with the marinade. (Alternatively, combine the tofu and marinade in a resealable bag.) Turn the tofu so that it's well coated. Let stand for at least 30 minutes and up to several hours, flipping periodically.

• Cut the eggplants in half lengthwise. Place in a colander, sprinkle with 2 teaspoons salt, and rub with your hands to ensure even distribution. Let stand for 25 to 30 minutes, while the tofu marinates.

• Slice the ginger into the thinnest possible rings. Place in a mortar along with the scallions, sesame seeds, sugar, and ¼ teaspoon salt. Use a pestle to pound the ginger until you get a pulpy mass, with some ragged pieces of ginger left intact. Add the lime juice. Stir in 1 tablespoon of the neutral-tasting oil. Taste and adjust the seasoning with more salt or sugar as necessary.

• Cook the couscous: Heat the remaining 1 tablespoon neutral-tasting oil in a deep skillet or saucepan over medium heat. Add the couscous and cook until fragrant and darkened a shade, 3 to 5 minutes. Stir in the boiling water and the remaining ¾ teaspoon salt, cover the pan and remove from the heat, and let stand for 10 minutes. Leave covered until ready to serve.

• Heat one side of a grill to a medium-high flame and grease the grates.

• Brush the eggplant with oil, then place it flesh side down on the grill, along with the corn, placing both over indirect heat (the cooler side of the grill). Cover the grill. Cook the eggplant for 5 to 10 minutes, until tender and easily pierced with a paring knife and char marks appear. Cook the corn for 5 to 7 minutes, turning every 2 to 3 minutes. Transfer to a plate to cool until safe to handle.

• If your grill is large enough, grill the tofu at the same time as the eggplant and corn. If not, place the tofu on the grill after the eggplant and corn are cooked, again over indirect heat, reserving any excess marinade. Cook for 4 to 6 minutes. Brush with a bit of the oil, then use a spatula to flip and cook the other side until it takes on grill marks. Baste with the leftover marinade. Transfer to a plate.

• Remove the kernels from the corn: Hold the corn upright or on its side on a large cutting board and, using a sharp chef's knife, slice off the kernels from one side in a single downward swipe. Work your way all the way around the cobs until you've trimmed off all the kernels.

• To serve, divide the couscous among four bowls. Top the couscous in each bowl with the eggplant, corn, tofu, and tomato. Top each serving with a spoonful of the ginger sauce and garnish with the basil or mint. This dish can be served warm or at room temperature.

zucchini "noodle" bowl

This is a simple and light bowl for a cool spring lunch or dinner, to be made when the farmers' market finally begins to generate some excitement, with thin asparagus, fiddlehead ferns, little carrots, and crisp baby turnips. This meal features a court bouillon–style broth, poached baby vegetables, soft-cooked eggs, and zucchini "noodles," a popular variation on flour-based noodles. The recipe benefits from planning ahead—the broth and eggs, for example, can be prepared in advance. And since the broth is relatively light and the vegetables are so simply prepared, the rich flavor and added body of a soft egg is a necessary component here. You can substitute the zucchini with udon, soba, somen, or another long, smooth noodle. SERVES 4

2 tablespoons good olive oil, plus more for drizzling

½ large or 1 small onion, diced

1 medium carrot, diced

2 celery stalks, diced

1 bay leaf

3 whole black peppercorns

Pinch of red pepper flakes

Pinch of fennel seeds

1 cup dry white wine

4 cups water

2 teaspoons fine sea salt

6 sprigs plus 1½ teaspoons minced fresh parsley

5 bushy sprigs plus ½ teaspoon minced fresh thyme

4 sprigs plus ½ teaspoon minced fresh tarragon

3 medium firm zucchini or yellow squash (about 2 pounds)

1½ to 2 pounds mixed baby spring vegetables, such as young carrots, snap peas, thin asparagus, baby turnips, or fiddlehead ferns, trimmed and cut into bite-sized pieces

4 large boiled eggs, molten yolk (page 224), or poached eggs (page 226)

• Heat the oil in a pot or medium saucepan over medium heat. Add the onion, diced carrot, celery, bay leaf, peppercorns, red pepper, and fennel seeds. Cook for about 5 minutes, stirring periodically, just until the vegetables begin to soften. Pour in the wine and water. Bring to

a simmer, add 1 teaspoon of the salt, then cook for 8 minutes. Add the sprigs of parsley, thyme, and tarragon and cook for 2 minutes more. Strain through a sieve or fine-mesh colander, discard the solids, and set the broth aside. The herb broth can be made up to 1 day in advance and stored, covered, in the refrigerator, or frozen for 1 to 2 months.

• Trim the ends off the zucchini, then, using a mandoline, julienne into long noodles about the size of linguini—between ¼ and ⅛ inch in thickness. The noodles can also be cut by hand: Slice the zucchini into long, thin slabs, then stack the slabs on top of each other and carefully cut into noodles. (Using a vegetable peeler in this case makes noodles that are too thin to hold up in the broth.) Toss with the remaining 1 teaspoon salt and let stand in a colander for 20 to 30 minutes. Gently squeeze to extract liquid.

• Bring a saucepan of salted water to a gentle boil. Add the spring vegetables in separate batches, and cook until just tender and easily pierced with a paring knife, then transfer each batch with a spider skimmer or slotted spoon to a plate. Carrots will take 3 to 5 minutes, thin asparagus 3 to 4 minutes, baby turnips 3 to 5 minutes, snap peas 1 to 2 minutes, and fiddle-heads 6 to 8 minutes.

• Bring the herb broth to a bare simmer. Taste, adding additional salt as necessary. Stir together the minced parsley, thyme, and tarragon in a small bowl.

• Using a strainer basket or sieve, dip the zucchini noodles into the vegetable cooking water or the broth to warm them, then divide among four bowls. Top with the baby vegetables. Split a soft-cooked egg over the vegetables in each bowl, cover each serving with about 1 cup broth, and garnish generously with the minced herbs. Drizzle with olive oil and serve immediately.

veggie burger bowl

MUSTARDY CHICKPEAS, BARLEY, PICKLES

If you'd told me when I was a teenager that I'd have devoted a good deal of my adult life to creating a veggie burger company, I never would have believed you. But to continue that trajectory, here's a burger bowl, with all the components of a bean-and-grain burger, deconstructed, plus some classic condiments. SERVES 4

1½ cups hulled or pearled barley or brown rice

1 teaspoon plus 1 pinch of fine sea salt

1¾ cups cooked chickpeas (one 15-ounce can, drained and rinsed)

¼ cup coarsely chopped fresh parsley or cilantro

2 tablespoons olive oil

1 tablespoon lemon juice

2 teaspoons Dijon mustard

Freshly ground black pepper

Heaping ¼ cup plain yogurt

2 to 4 teaspoons sriracha, Chili-Garlic Sambal (page 241 or store-bought), or *gochujang* (see page 37)

1 cup halved cherry tomatoes

1 avocado, diced

½ cup Quick Cucumber Pickles (page 231) or favorite store-bought pickles, sliced

⅓ cup Pickled Red Onions (page 230)

2 cups shredded lettuce (such as butter leaf, watercress, or arugula), or 1 cup sprouts

• Soak hulled barley in water for at least 4 hours or up to overnight (pearled barley doesn't need to be soaked). Rinse and drain, then transfer to a saucepan and cover with 3 inches of water. Bring to a boil and add 1 teaspoon of the salt. Reduce the heat to a simmer, partially cover the pan, and cook until chewy-tender, 30 to 40 minutes, or 20 to 30 minutes for pearled. Drain thoroughly and return to the saucepan. (If using brown rice, follow the cooking instructions on page 222.)

• Meanwhile, combine the chickpeas with the parsley or cilantro, oil, lemon juice, mustard, a big pinch of salt, and several grinds of pepper. Let marinate for at least 20 minutes. In a separate bowl, whisk together the yogurt and sriracha, *sambal*, or *gochujang* to taste.

• To serve, divide the barley or rice among four bowls, then arrange the marinated chickpeas, tomatoes, avocado, pickles, pickled onions, and lettuce or sprouts over each serving. Top with a dollop of the sriracha yogurt and serve.

cauliflower "couscous" bowl

A few pan-fried tofu matchsticks, crisp shavings of radish and celery, tender baby arugula, tart bursts of pomegranate seeds, and a shower of fresh herbs make for a very fresh vegetable-centric bowl for almost any time of the year. This method for transforming cauliflower into something that resembles couscous has become increasingly popular. Its fluffy texture and soft flavor makes an easy base for any number of toppings and I especially enjoy it as part of the next day's lunch, served cold. The barely sweetened savory seed brittle is addictive—it makes extra, and you'll find other uses for it in salads, soups, or even as a replacement for granola. SERVES 4

for the savory seed brittle

1 egg white

2 teaspoons maple syrup

1 tablespoon sugar

3/4 teaspoon ground cinnamon

1/4 teaspoon fine sea salt

Pinch of cayenne pepper

1/2 cup raw pumpkin seeds

1/2 cup raw sunflower seeds

3 tablespoons toasted sesame seeds

1 1/2 teaspoons toasted whole coriander seeds, coarsely crushed

1 1/2 teaspoons toasted cumin seeds, coarsely crushed

1 teaspoon whole black peppercorns, coarsely crushed

for the cauliflower bowls

1/4 teaspoon salt

2 tablespoons red wine vinegar

1 medium head cauliflower (about 1 1/2 pounds), cut into small florets

2 small shallots, minced

1 tablespoon neutral-tasting oil

7 ounces firm tofu (half of a 14-ounce block), sliced and pressed (see page 119)

5 cups loosely packed baby arugula

2 crisp celery stalks, thinly sliced on the bias

6 radishes, sliced into thin rounds

1/2 cup pomegranate seeds

1/4 cup loosely packed fresh mint leaves

Olive oil, for drizzling

- Make the brittle: Preheat the oven to 300°F.

- In a mixing bowl, beat the egg white until frothy. Whisk in the maple syrup, sugar, cinnamon, salt, and cayenne. Stir in the pumpkin and sunflower seeds. Transfer to a baking dish or oven-safe skillet with a slotted spoon, leaving any liquid behind in the bowl. Transfer to the oven and bake for 20 minutes. Sprinkle the sesame seeds, coriander seeds, cumin seeds, and peppercorns over the mixture, stir once, and bake for 10 to 15 minutes more, until golden. Cool and then break up into small pieces. Stored in an airtight container, the brittle will keep for about 5 days.

- Make the cauliflower bowls: Stir together the vinegar and salt in a small bowl until the salt dissolves.

- Place the cauliflower in a food processor and pulse until broken down into a fine, couscous-like consistency, stopping to scrape down the sides periodically. Bring about ½ inch of water to a simmer in a small saucepan. Add the cauliflower, cover the pan, and cook for 2 to 4 minutes, until just tender. Drain in a fine-mesh colander. Wipe the pan dry, then return the cauliflower to it. Stir in the salted vinegar and the shallots.

- Meanwhile, heat the neutral-tasting oil in a nonstick skillet over medium heat. Add the tofu, arranging it in a single layer, and cook for 3 to 5 minutes without disturbing, until golden brown. Flip and repeat on the other side. Transfer to a paper towel–lined plate to drain and sprinkle with a pinch of salt, then cut into matchsticks.

- To serve, divide the arugula and cauliflower "couscous" among four bowls. Top with the tofu, celery, radishes, pomegranate seeds, mint, and a generous handful of the brittle. Drizzle each serving with olive oil and serve.

a few knife tips

Vegetarian cooking requires a fair amount of knife work. There's no need to be a virtuoso, but a comfortable command of a standard chef's knife will help you to work more quickly and uniformly. This is especially true if you're accustomed to using a paring knife or anything smaller than an 8-inch chef's knife for all your slicing and dicing. I always recommend taking a knife skills class for cooks of all skill levels—lots of kitchenware stores, culinary schools, and continuing education programs offer them. Even for skilled cooks, a refresher course is helpful. Here are a few very brief tips and guidelines.

CHOKE UP ON THE KNIFE. Grip it where the blade meets the handle. Your thumb and index finger hold the blade itself, and the rest of your hand wraps around the bolster and handle of the knife. This allows your wrist to be the fulcrum so that your arm doesn't have to do too much work, and also allows you to have much more control over the blade. You may develop a blister or two while you're getting used to this grip.

TUCK, TUCK, TUCK! All of the fingers of your other hand—your secondary hand— should be tucked under, securing the food that's being cut up, almost as if gripping a tennis ball, none splaying out. (The ring finger of my secondary hand has a terrible habit of sliding out from the tucked grip, and it's no surprise that it is the one that's suffered repeated damage.)

USE THE SECONDARY HAND TO GUIDE. Holding your secondary hand correctly, your fingers should stand mostly perpendicular to the board. With a sturdy grip on the knife, and working slowly to start, let the side of the knife rub against the knuckle of the tucked fingers. This allows the knuckle to *guide* the cut. Move the secondary hand after the cut's been made to the point where it will act as guide for the next one. Repeat.

SLICE FORWARD, RATHER THAN DOWNWARD. The tip of the knife should touch the cutting board most of the time you're using the knife. Let the knife scoop back and forth, making forward rocking motions on the board as it slices. Don't lift it fully into the air and make the cuts downward. This is dangerous and tiring on your arm.

Here are two types of cuts frequently used in this book:

TO SHRED LETTUCE, KALE, LARGE-LEAFED HERBS, AND OTHER GREENS: Make a stack of the leaves, then gently roll them up into a cigar. Set the rolled-up greens lengthwise on your cutting board and, using your secondary hand to guide, cut the rolled greens into very thin ribbons. This is how to chiffonade—slice into thin wisps—herbs like basil and mint.

TO JULIENNE VEGETABLES LIKE CUCUMBERS, RADISHES, OR PEELED GINGER: This is a two-part process. First, carefully slice the vegetables into thin rounds. Then make small stacks and slice into matchsticks, such that their height and width are the same. This same method works well for dicing—simply turn the matchsticks 90 degrees and cut them into small squares.

Lastly, no matter how expensive your knife, it's important to care for it properly. Hand-wash immediately after you're done—don't put it in the dishwasher—then wipe it dry and store it in a protective plastic sleeve, on a wall-mounted magnetic strip, or in whatever other way prevents the sharp edge from getting dinged up in a cluttered drying rack or drawer. Run it over a carbon steel every few times you use it—some cooks advocate doing this every time, but I can't keep up with that—and then have it professionally sharpened every 8 months to a year. With proper care, a good knife will last decades, if not a lifetime.

rutabaga fried rice

This is the kind of easy fried rice dish that I make all year long—a reason to look forward to leftover rice. Rutabaga has become my favorite of the limited Northeast winter vegetable options—I love its ruddy, purple-hued skin, and the bright, sweet aroma of the flesh, which, when cooked, gives way to a sophisticated, round flavor that falls somewhere between a turnip and a golden beet. Rutabagas are especially good when cooked crisp and, as in this fried rice, are complemented by an Asian flavor profile. Rounded out with some greens and a fried egg, this is a rewarding, decadent, and quick meal. As with my other fried rice recipes, avoid over-crowding the pan—this recipe is only for two. SERVES 2

2 tablespoons neutral-tasting oil

1 medium rutabaga (12 to 16 ounces), peeled and cut into ½-inch cubes

1 small onion, sliced into thin strips

1 teaspoon toasted sesame oil

1 teaspoon minced garlic

1 teaspoon grated fresh ginger

2½ cups day-old cooked white or brown rice or mixed grains (pages 221, 222, and 223)

¼ teaspoon fine sea salt

¼ teaspoon sugar

1 tablespoon soy sauce, plus more for serving

3 cups baby greens, like baby kale, spinach, or tatsoi

2 large soft- or crispy-fried eggs (page 225)

½ cup crunchy sprouts, such as sunflower sprouts, pea shoots, or mung bean sprouts

Quick Cucumber Pickles (optional; page 231)

Sriracha or Chili-Garlic Sambal (page 241 or store-bought), for serving

• Heat 1 tablespoon of the neutral-tasting oil in a wide nonstick skillet over medium-high heat. Add the rutabaga and spread it into a single layer. Cook for about 4 minutes, undisturbed, until the bottom sides are crisp and browned. Flip and cook for another 4 minutes, until crisp and browned on another side. Test doneness with a paring knife—the rutabaga should be tender and fall off the knife, but not mushy. Transfer to a plate with a slotted spoon. Wipe out the skillet.

• Return the skillet to the heat and add the remaining 1 tablespoon neutral-tasting oil. Once hot, add the onion. Cook without disturbing for 3 to 4 minutes, until it takes on some color around the edges and softens slightly. Stir in the sesame oil, then the garlic and ginger, and cook, stirring periodically, until fragrant. Add the rice, salt, and sugar, crumbling the rice with your hands into the skillet or breaking it up with a spatula. Stir constantly, tossing and flipping until the rice begins to appear translucent and slightly crisp and the pan is dry, 4 to 5 minutes. Scoop out a space in the middle of the pan and pour in the soy sauce. Let it bubble for a few moments, then stir into the rice. When the pan is dry again, after 3 to 5 minutes, add the greens and stir until wilted. Remove from the heat.

• Divide the fried rice among two bowls, and top the rice in each bowl with the rutabaga, a fried egg, the sprouts, and the pickles, if using. Pass the hot sauce and additional soy sauce at the table.

toasted bulgur bowl

CHICKPEAS, SUMMER VEGETABLES, TAHINI DRIZZLE

Bulgur—parboiled cracked wheat—is best known as the primary ingredient in the Middle Eastern salad tabbouleh. I love its toasty flavor and chewy texture, and its quick-cooking properties are a boon. Here I fold chopped blanched greens and parsley into the bulgur, which gives it a tabbouleh-like appearance, and then I go bold with textures and flavors: tomatoes, cucumbers, chickpeas, and almonds, an assertive tahini drizzle, and a finish of torn mint leaves. It's a hearty, healthy vegan bowl, bright, crunchy, and juicy, and great for packed lunches on road trips and picnics. Quinoa is a fine substitute for the bulgur; just refer to the cooking method on page 210, as it can't be soaked as bulgur can. SERVES 4

1½ cups coarse bulgur

Boiling water

1 large bunch Swiss chard, spinach, or kale (about 12 ounces)

1 cup coarsely chopped fresh parsley

2 medium Kirby cucumbers

¼ cup well-stirred tahini

3 tablespoons lemon juice

1 teaspoon minced garlic

1 teaspoon ground cumin

½ teaspoon fine sea salt

¼ cup water, plus more as needed

2 cups halved cherry tomatoes or diced ripe tomatoes

1¾ cups cooked chickpeas (one 15-ounce can, drained and rinsed)

¼ cup chopped roasted almonds

Good-quality olive oil, for drizzling

⅓ cup torn fresh mint leaves, for garnish

Finishing salt, for garnish

Lemon wedges, for serving

• Spread out the bulgur in a wide skillet and place over medium heat. Toast, swirling the pan frequently, until fragrant and the bulgur has darkened a shade, 5 to 7 minutes. Tip into a heat-proof bowl and add enough boiling water to cover the bulgur by 2 inches. Cover with a lid, plate, or piece of plastic wrap and let stand for 10 to 20 minutes, until chewy-tender. Drain through a fine-mesh sieve, pressing on the grains with a spatula to extract excess liquid. Return to the bowl and allow to cool.

• Trim the tough stems of the chard, kale, or mature spinach and discard. Bring a saucepan of salted water to boil and prepare an ice-water bath. Add the greens and cook until wilted, 1 to 3 minutes. Transfer to the ice-water bath, then drain and squeeze out the excess water with your hands. Chop the greens finely, then stir into the bulgur along with the parsley.

• Halve the cucumbers lengthwise and scoop out the seeds with a spoon. Cut into ½-inch-thick wedges.

• Whisk together the tahini, lemon juice, garlic, cumin, salt, and water. Add additional water by the tablespoon until a relatively thin, pourable consistency is reached.

• To serve, divide the bulgur among four bowls, then top with the cucumbers, tomatoes, chickpeas, and almonds. Drizzle about 2 tablespoons of tahini dressing over each bowl, followed by a light drizzle of olive oil, then garnish each bowl with the mint and a pinch of finishing salt. Serve with the lemon wedges.

black rice burrito bowl

Marinated black beans, cool avocado, sweet mango, a good helping of herbs, tangy pickled onions, and the soft, toasty flavor of pepitas (pumpkin seeds) combine for a dramatically colorful presentation. Delicate and chewy, black rice—also called "forbidden rice"—is a purple-hued, unpolished variety that touts many of the same health benefits as brown rice, but with a nubbier texture. And like brown rice, it benefits from soaking for a few hours, which makes its nutrients more accessible and also shortens its cooking time. Like all nuts and seeds, pepitas' flavor fades as they sit, so it's best to toast them just before serving, as instructed below. SERVES 4

1½ cups black rice

2½ cups water, plus more for soaking the rice

2 teaspoons cumin seeds

1¾ cups cooked black or pinto beans (or one 15-ounce can, rinsed)

2 serrano chilies, seeded and finely diced

3 tablespoons olive oil

Juice of 2 limes (about 3 tablespoons), plus lime wedges for serving

¾ teaspoon chili powder

¾ teaspoon fine sea salt

¼ cup raw pumpkin seeds

1 avocado, diced

1 mango, diced

1 cup shredded purple cabbage

½ cup Pickled Red Onions (page 230)

¼ cup crumbled mild white cheese, such as cotija or queso fresco, feta, or ricotta salata (optional)

¼ cup loosely packed fresh cilantro leaves and tender stems

2 tablespoons loosely packed fresh oregano leaves

Pico de gallo (store-bought or homemade, see page 152), for serving

• Place the rice in a medium bowl, cover with about 3 inches of water, and soak for 2 to 12 hours. Rinse, then place in a saucepan and cover with plenty of cold water. Place over high heat and bring the water to a boil. Cook for 15 to 25 minutes, until the rice is tender. Drain through a sieve, then return to the pot and let stand, covered, until ready to serve. (If you skip the soaking step, you'll need to continue cooking the rice for an additional 5 to 10 minutes.)

pico de gallo

Pico de gallo shouldn't be watery. Seeding the tomatoes cuts back on the liquid content, but as it sits it'll accumulate more. Just pour off most of the liquid before serving. Fresh salsas like this are best eaten within a day or two of making them. MAKES ABOUT 1 CUP

2 ripe, medium tomatoes (about 1 pound)

1 small or ½ large white onion, diced

1 serrano chili, seeded if desired, finely diced

½ cup coarsely chopped fresh cilantro

1 to 2 tablespoons lime juice

½ teaspoon fine sea salt

• Core the tomatoes and cut into quarters, then slice each quarter in half. Carefully trim out and discard the seeds. Finely dice the tomatoes.

• In a medium bowl, combine the tomatoes, onion, chili, cilantro, lime juice, and salt. Taste and add additional lime juice, salt, or chili as needed.

• Meanwhile, heat a small skillet over medium heat. Add the cumin seeds and toast for 45 to 90 seconds, until fragrant. Transfer to a mortar or spice mill and coarsely grind.

• Combine the beans, cumin, serrano chilies, oil, lime juice, chili powder, and salt in a mixing bowl. Let stand as the rice cooks.

• Return the skillet to the heat and add the pumpkin seeds. Toast, swirling the pan often, for 3 to 5 minutes, until the seeds turn a pale brown color and start to pop. Transfer to a plate or bowl.

• To serve, divide the rice among four bowls, then spoon the beans over the rice in each bowl. Top each serving with the avocado, mango, cabbage, pickled onions, pumpkin seeds, cheese, if using, cilantro, and oregano. Serve with lime wedges and pico de gallo on the side.

mujadara bowl

This dish is my adaptation of *mujadara*, the savory Middle Eastern dish of lentils, rice, and fried onions. Summer squash, when cooked properly, can be a real treat, and here it offers some succulence that contrasts beautifully with the crisp lettuce—hydroponic varieties work especially well, since they usually have excellent crisp texture—cool yogurt, salty onions, and earthy base of lentils and grains. I've omitted all of the dried spices typically associated with mujadara—cinnamon, cumin, allspice—and used grassy-flavored quinoa instead of rice. (You can use medium-grain white rice if you wish.) Be sure to use the flat green or brown lentils, rather than the smaller dark green (du puy) or black ones; the lentils and grains must share the same cooking time, and the small, denser varieties take too long. SERVES 4

1 pound small, firm summer squash (2 or 3)

2½ teaspoons plus a few pinches of salt

4 tablespoons neutral-tasting oil

1 small onion, peeled and sliced into very thin rings

1 cup quinoa or medium-grain white rice

2 teaspoons minced garlic

1 cup brown or green lentils, rinsed and picked through

3½ cups water

2 cups shredded crisp lettuce, such as butter leaf, Boston, romaine, or iceberg

½ cup chopped toasted walnuts or sliced almonds

¼ cup plain yogurt

¼ cup torn fresh mint leaves, for garnish

Lemon wedges, for serving

• Trim the ends off the squash, then dice into ½-inch cubes. Toss with 2 teaspoons of the salt and place in a colander to drain for 20 to 30 minutes. Gently pat dry with a clean kitchen towel or paper towels.

- Heat 3 tablespoons of the oil in a wide saucepan over medium heat. Add the onion and cook, stirring, until golden brown and crispy, 15 to 20 minutes. Watch carefully during the last few minutes, as the onion can burn easily. Use a slotted spoon to transfer to a paper towel–lined plate, leaving the oil in the pan, and sprinkle the onion with a few pinches of salt.

- Return the pan to the heat. Stir in the quinoa and cook, stirring frequently, for 3 to 4 minutes, until aromatic and the pan is dry. Stir in the garlic, followed by the lentils and the water. Bring to a boil, add the remaining ½ teaspoon salt, reduce the heat to low, cover the pan, and cook for 17 to 20 minutes, until the quinoa and lentils are tender and the water is absorbed. If the lentils and grains are cooked before all the water is absorbed, simply drain the excess. Remove from the heat and let stand until ready to serve.

- Heat the remaining 1 tablespoon oil in a wide skillet over medium heat. Add half of the squash, or as much as you can fit in an uncrowded, single layer. Cook, turning periodically, until golden brown on a few sides but still tender in the centers, 3 to 6 minutes—overcooking here will result in mushy squash, so taste frequently and watch closely. Use the slotted spoon to transfer to a plate, then add the remaining squash to the pan and repeat.

- Divide the hot quinoa-lentil mixture among four bowls. Top each serving with the lettuce, squash, nuts, dollops of yogurt, and onions. Garnish with the mint and serve with the lemon wedges on the side.

buckwheat bowl

Buckwheat contains no wheat, and it's not technically a grain either. It's a fruit seed related to rhubarb, and is loaded with all kinds of healthful properties, including an abundance of minerals like zinc, copper, and manganese, and a decent amount of protein. When the groats are roasted to a darker, purplish shade, they're known as kasha, a staple of Eastern European cuisine. It has a distinctively nutty and almost fruity aroma, but is amenable to lots of textures and flavors. I like it here as the base for roasted fennel and mushrooms, wisps of celery, and yogurt. Pomegranate molasses, which is increasingly available at grocery stores and specialty markets, lends a dark tanginess that pairs well with the yogurt. I sometimes cap this bowl with a poached egg. Don't overcook the buckwheat—it will become both dry and mushy at the same time. SERVES 4

1 large or 2 small fennel bulbs (about 1 pound) plus 2 tablespoons chopped fronds

8 ounces shiitake mushrooms, stems discarded

4 tablespoons olive oil, plus more for drizzling

1 teaspoon fine sea salt, plus more for sprinkling

Freshly ground black pepper

1 small onion, minced

2 teaspoons minced garlic

1½ cups buckwheat groats or kasha

3 cups water

2 stalks celery

4 large boiled eggs, molten yolk (page 224), or poached eggs (page 226), optional

½ cup plain yogurt

4 teaspoons pomegranate molasses

• Preheat the oven to 375°F.

• If still attached, trim off and discard the stalks from the fennel bulb(s), then cut the bulb(s) in half lengthwise. Use a paring knife to cut out the core from each half, then slice the fennel into ½-inch-thick strips, as you would an onion. Arrange on a baking sheet. Arrange the mushrooms in a single layer on a separate baking sheet.

• Divide 3 tablespoons of the oil over the mushrooms and fennel, sprinkle with salt and pepper, and transfer to the oven. Roast the mushrooms until soft, juicy, and caramelized around the edges, 15 to 20 minutes. Roast the fennel until very tender and caramelized, 30 to 40 minutes.

• Meanwhile, heat the remaining 1 tablespoon oil in a large saucepan or deep skillet over medium heat. Add the onion and cook, stirring periodically, until softened and translucent, 5 to 7 minutes. Stir in the garlic, then add the buckwheat groats or kasha and cook, stirring constantly, until fragrant, about 2 minutes. Pour in the water, bring to a boil, and add 1 teaspoon salt. Reduce the heat to low, cover the pan, and cook until the liquid is absorbed. If the groats are tender before all the liquid is absorbed, remove the pan from the heat and drain off the liquid. Buckwheat groats will take 15 to 20 minutes; kasha will take less time, 10 to 15 minutes. Taste frequently to prevent overcooking. Fluff with a fork and stir in a little freshly ground black pepper. Taste and add more salt as necessary. Keep the pan covered until ready to serve.

• Just before serving, slice the celery into paper-thin shavings on a steep bias.

• Divide the hot buckwheat among four bowls. Top with the roasted fennel, mushrooms, celery, and split soft-boiled or poached eggs, if using. Dollop each serving with yogurt, drizzle with pomegranate molasses and olive oil, garnish with the reserved fennel fronds, and serve.

sprouted lentil bowl

POACHED EGGS, APPLES, CILANTRO SAUCE

Sprouted lentils, when quickly blanched, have a light, fluffy texture that belies how hearty and nutritious they are. Making them does require some advance planning—two to three days—but you can use one of the packaged bean sprout medleys available in the produce section of the grocery store in place of home-made ones, or cook lentils the usual way by covering with water in a pan, bringing it to a simmer, cooking until just tender, and then draining. In this recipe, they're paired with a green sauce in which the zingy flavors of cilantro, vinegar, and lime make the heat of the fresh chilies secondary. SERVES 4

1⅓ cup green lentils

4 cups filtered water

2½ cups packed coarsely chopped fresh cilantro leaves and tender stems

1 serrano chili, seeded if desired and coarsely chopped

Juice of 1 lime

1½ teaspoons white vinegar

1 small garlic clove

½ teaspoon fine sea salt

5 cups tender salad greens

4 large poached eggs (page 226) or boiled eggs, molten yolk (page 224)

8 small radishes, thinly sliced

1 tart, crisp apple, cored and cut into matchsticks or small dice

½ cup Pickled Red Onions (page 230)

¼ cup hulled and toasted sunflower seeds or Tamari Sunflower Seeds (page 205)

4 tablespoons olive oil

Flaky salt

Freshly ground black pepper

• To sprout the lentils: Rinse them well, then place in a wide-mouth glass jar. Cover with the filtered water. Top the jar with a piece of fine mesh or a few layers of cheesecloth secured with a rubber band or the jar ring. Let stand overnight in a warm place. The next day, drain the lentils, rinse, and then return to the jar. Secure the mesh or cheesecloth lid. Set two flat, short objects—two plastic lids or square-handled chopsticks work well—inside a baking pan, flip the jars upside down then place it so that it's balanced on top of those two objects. This sounds very fussy, but the purpose is so air flows beneath the jar and the liquid that drains off doesn't collect inside the jar. Let stand for 12 hours.

• Rinse the lentils, return them to the jar, secure the lid, and repeat. Repeat this two or three times more, until you see sprouts ¼ to ½ inch long. Make sure that the sprouts are thoroughly dry (gently blot them with a paper towel if necessary), then transfer to a container to store in the refrigerator and use within 3 days.

• Combine 2 cups of the cilantro with the serrano, lime juice, vinegar, garlic, and sea salt in a small food processor or the plastic cup that usually comes with an immersion blender. Puree until smooth, adding water by the teaspoon until you have a fairly thin, pourable consistency— about that of hot sauce.

• Bring a saucepan of water to boil and salt it generously. Add the sprouted lentils and cook for 60 to 90 seconds, until just tender. Drain thoroughly.

• Divide the lentils and salad greens among three bowls. Top each serving with 1 egg and about 1 tablespoon of the cilantro sauce. Divide the remaining ½ cup cilantro leaves, the radishes, apple, pickled onions, and sunflower seeds on top. Drizzle each serving with 1 tablespoon olive oil, sprinkle with the flaky salt and black pepper, and serve.

farro bowl

Farro—a grain similar to but not the same as barley, emmer, and spelt—has a good deal of substance. Rich and creamy things, such as the ricotta amped up with pesto in this recipe, are complementary. Use a good, fresh-made ricotta that's light and fluffy, rather than grainy and dense. For the vegetables, instead of the carrots, beans, and potatoes here, asparagus and snap peas are terrific, as are chunks of ripe tomato, summer squash, roasted winter squash, or any type of leftover roasted vegetables. Lastly, farro shouldn't be added straight to boiling water, or the insides will split the husks open. Cover it with cold water and place over the heat so that the grains heat up gradually, and the result will be much more attractive. SERVES 4

2 cups farro

2 teaspoons fine sea salt

1 tablespoon sherry vinegar

Pinch of red pepper flakes

8 ounces small to medium carrots of different colors

6 ounces green beans

8 ounces small waxy potatoes

6 small-to-medium radishes

½ cup fresh ricotta

3 tablespoons Pesto (page 163)

Olive oil, as needed and for drizzling

½ cup chopped toasted walnuts

¼ cup coarsely chopped fresh basil or parsley, for garnish

Flaky salt, for garnish

Freshly ground black pepper, for garnish

Lemon wedges, for garnish

• Place the farro in a medium or large saucepan and cover with at least 6 cups water. Bring to a boil, add the sea salt, then reduce the heat to a gentle boil and cook for 16 to 20 minutes, until the farro is tender but retains a pleasant chew. Drain, then return to the pot and toss with the vinegar and red pepper flakes. Let stand, covered, until ready to serve.

• Meanwhile, prepare the vegetables. Peel the carrots and slice into ½-inch-thick rounds. Trim

the stem ends off the green beans. Slice the potatoes into ½-inch-thick rounds or quarter them if they're small. Cut the radishes into paper-thin rounds.

• Fill a saucepan or pot with about ½ inch water, then fit with a steamer unit. Bring the water to a simmer. Steam carrots, green beans, and potatoes in separate batches, or in separate layers of a stacking steamer unit, until tender and easily pierced with a paring knife. The carrots will take 4 to 6 minutes, the string beans 1 to 3 minutes, and the potatoes 4 to 7 minutes. Transfer the vegetables to a plate and cover loosely with a piece of foil to keep them warm.

• Stir together the ricotta and pesto until smooth. Add olive oil, about a teaspoon at a time as needed to thin it out; the mixture should be light and fluffy. Taste and add pinches of salt as needed.

• To serve, divide the cooked farro among four bowls. Top the farro in each bowl with the steamed vegetables, radishes, and walnuts. Top with about 2 tablespoons of the pesto ricotta per bowl, then garnish each serving with the basil or parsley, a drizzle of olive oil, a pinch of flaky salt, a few grinds of pepper, and a lemon wedge.

• After the grains and the vegetables have cooled completely, this bowl can be assembled in airtight containers and stored in the refrigerator for 2 or 3 days. It's great for packed lunches and picnics.

pesto

Basil, pine nuts, and Parmesan cheese are traditional, but you can change up the greens and nuts however you please. Arugula, mint, spinach, even steamed hearty greens like kale are all good here, and walnuts, almonds, or Brazil nuts each add a slightly different flavor profile. Play around.

MAKES ABOUT 1 CUP

1/4 cup toasted pine nuts, walnuts, or almonds

1 garlic clove, chopped

Lemon juice to taste

1/4 teaspoon fine sea salt

1 cup packed fresh basil leaves

3 to 4 tablespoons olive oil

3 tablespoons grated Parmesan cheese

Freshly ground black pepper

• Place the nuts, garlic, a squeeze of lemon juice, and the salt in the bowl of a food processor and pulse until coarsely combined. Add the basil, pulsing a few times to incorporate. With the motor running, add the oil one tablespoon at a time until a smooth, thick consistency is achieved. Stir in the cheese and several grinds of black pepper, then taste, adjusting the seasonings as needed. It will keep for up to a week in the fridge, and can be frozen for a few months.

dumpling bowls

I first encountered the concept of a dumpling bowl at Rickshaw, a casual midtown Manhattan restaurant that started out as a food truck (sadly, they've since closed). At Rickshaw, eight or so different dumplings were on offer every day, and customers could choose to have them à la carte, as part of a soup, or over a salad. I found the soup and salad versions to be especially satisfying. In the winter, the soups warmed me up; in the summer, the salads were cool and refreshing; and in both cases, I left happy and full, ready to carry on with my day.

I use filled and folded Chinese- and Japanese-style dumplings as the focal point of these meals-in-a-bowl. As with the other recipes in this book, I've taken liberties with the dumpling fillings, drawing not just from traditional ingredients and flavor profiles, but also from pantry staples and the bounty of the farmers' market to create dishes like Chickpea Potstickers, Rich Lentil Dumplings, Spicy Carrot Dumplings, Parsnip Dumplings, and Summer Squash Dumplings. To round them out, each recipe recommends different possible pairings, including two soups, a versatile green salad, a quinoa and kale bowl, or rice and stir-fried Asian greens.

The base elements are quick and easy, but making dumplings does require a bit of a time investment for the shaping process. Plan on spending a stretch of time in the kitchen—a weekend afternoon, or a slow evening—stocking your freezer with a batch or two of dumplings. Or, how about a little pop-up dumpling factory? Home-made dumplings are a great excuse for an interactive food party—cook up a few different fillings before your guests arrive, then gather around the table with all the necessary supplies, offer a quick tutorial, and let everyone join in.

The dumpling recipes here yield 25 to 30 dumplings, which is a little more than what you'll need to serve four people with the bowl pairings. Just keep any extras in the freezer for later bowls or for easy snacking. Because once they're on hand, they can be cooked straight out of the freezer in less than 5 minutes. All that's left to do is to throw together a salad, or cook some rice and stir-fry some greens. It's a great, healthy way to plan ahead for busy weeknight cooking. You might even repurpose this dumpling-bowl concept by subbing in store-bought frozen dumplings for home-made ones. That's fine; I don't judge.

dumplings

a few dumpling shapes

I take classes on dumplings whenever I can, because as wonderful as written instructions are, hands-on guidance makes a world of difference. If you see a class listing, sign up for it! But if that's not an option, give these instructions and photos some scrutiny, perhaps check online for video tutorials, then head straight into your kitchen and get to work. You'll get the hang of it, and once you slip into the rhythm, it goes quickly. You may even find yourself entering a meditative state.

Here are instructions for how to shape a few basic dumplings, as well as some slightly more fussy dumplings and pleated potstickers. Don't fret over misshapen dumplings. They're edible no matter how they look; it's what's on the inside that counts.

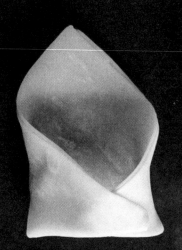

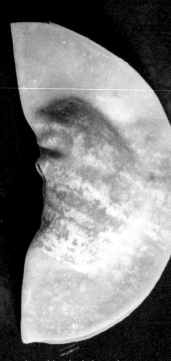

"NURSES' CAP" DUMPLINGS

This shape can be steamed, boiled, or fried. If you are frying them, use thicker dumpling wrappers. Place about 2 teaspoons filling in the center of a square dumpling wrapper. Fold into a triangle shape as instructed for Half Moons or Triangles. Lay the triangle on your work surface with the longest edge closest to you. Moisten the left or right corner of the triangle, then join the opposite corners by looping them around the filling and pressing them together to seal.

HALF MOONS OR TRIANGLES

This is the easiest dumpling shape for steamed and boiled dumplings. Place about 2 teaspoons filling in the center of a square or round dumpling wrapper. Moisten half of the perimeter or two edges of the wrapper, and fold the dry area over the moist, sealing the two parts together and gently pressing out as much air as possible. You'll have shaped the dumplings into either half moons, if using round skins, or triangles, if using square ones.

PLEATED POTSTICKERS

These dumplings require the most practice, but are the most satisfying to master. They can be steamed or boiled, but are best when pan-fried.

Place about 2 teaspoons filling in the center of a round, thicker-style dumpling wrapper. Moisten half of the perimeter. Hold up the dumpling in your dominant hand by two edges, with the moistened side facing the unmoistened side, so that you're looking at the front-facing part of the dumpling wrapper rather than into the filling. To start, it may be easiest to let the dumpling rest on your work surface, so that you can use both hands to seal the dumpling, but once you get the hang of it, you'll use your dominant hand, the same one holding the dumpling, to guide the sealing as you seal with your opposite hand. Tuck three pleats down the left side of the front-facing dumpling wrapper, pointing the pleats left and pressing them onto the back-facing part of the dumpling wrapper as you go. Now do the same to the right side, making pleats down and pointing them to the right, sealing the whole parcel together. Flatten the bottom of the dumpling on your work surface and tuck the ends back slightly, so that it sits upright with the pleats pointing at a roughly 45 degree angle.

BUNCHED WONTONS

This is another easy shape for boiled and steamed dumplings. Make sure to seek out larger, thin, square dumpling wrappers, at least 4 inches in width (you can also trim down spring-roll sheets, or roll out a stack of two small wrappers with a rolling pin, dusting them with flour or cornstarch as you go). Place about 2 teaspoons filling in the center of the dumpling wrapper. Moisten all the exposed area of the dumpling wrapper, then gather it around the filling and bunch it up like a little parcel.

SHUMAI

Japanese shumai dumplings aren't sealed, as the others in this book are (I think of them as "open-faced" dumplings), which makes them a little quicker to assemble. They should only be steamed.

Place about 2 teaspoons filling in the center of a thin, square dumpling wrapper. Moisten most of the exposed wrapper, then gather it up around the filling, leaving the excess dumpling wrapper sticking up rustically and the filling exposed in the center. Wrap your thumb and index finger around the filling to secure it, then flatten the dumpling's base on your work surface, so that it stands upright.

edamame dumplings

These springy dumplings manage to be both rich and light at the same time—the toasted sesame oil and sesame seeds add the richness, and edamame and refreshing mint contribute lightness. I like them best steamed, and for quickest assembly I usually make half-moons or triangles, though they work well in any shape. Drizzled with a simple, vinegary soy dressing (the honey-soy dressing on page 204, for example) or even a sweet soy sauce like *kecap manis*, these also make an easy starter or side dish, eaten with chopsticks. MAKES 25 TO 30 DUMPLINGS

1½ cups frozen shelled edamame

¼ cup grated carrot

1 tablespoon neutral-tasting oil

1 teaspoon toasted sesame oil

1 teaspoon brown rice vinegar

½ teaspoon fine sea salt

¼ teaspoon sugar

2 scallions, white and green parts, thinly sliced

2 tablespoons chopped fresh mint

1 teaspoon toasted sesame seeds

25 to 30 thin round or square dumpling wrappers

for the bowls

Fragrant Wonton Soup (page 203) or Green Salad with Honey-Soy Vinaigrette (page 204)

• Bring a saucepan of water to boil and salt it generously. Add the frozen edamame to the saucepan and cook for 3 to 5 minutes, or according to package instructions, until just tender. During the last 20 seconds of cooking, add the carrot. Drain through a fine-mesh sieve and rinse well under cold running water until cool. Drain thoroughly.

• Combine the edamame and carrot in the bowl of a food processor with the neutral-tasting oil, sesame oil, vinegar, salt, and sugar. Pulse several times until a chunky filling forms, being careful not to overprocess. Add the scallions, mint, and sesame seeds and pulse a few times more to incorporate them. Taste, adding more salt or vinegar as needed.

• Set up your dumpling assembly station: Place a stack of dumpling wrappers on one end of a cutting board and cover with a lightly moistened towel or paper towel to prevent them from drying out. Place a small bowl of water and the dumpling filling within reach. Also set out a parchment-lined baking sheet and moistened clean towel for the assembled dumplings.

• Fill and shape the dumplings into half moons or triangles, nurses' caps, or bunched wontons (see page 168), arranging them on the baking sheet as you go and covering with the towel to prevent them from drying out. If you're not eating them immediately, place the tray in the freezer for 30 minutes, until the dumplings are firmed up, then transfer to an airtight container or resealable bag and keep them in the freezer until ready to serve.

• **To steam the dumplings:** Heat ½ inch of water in a skillet until simmering. Use a paper towel moistened with a bit of oil to lightly grease the layers of a stacking steamer unit, then arrange the fresh or frozen dumplings inside so that they're not touching. Place the steamer in the simmering water. Cook for 3 minutes if the dumplings are fresh, or 5 minutes if frozen. Use caution when opening the steamer, as a cloud of very hot steam will rush out.

• **To boil the dumplings:** With the soup at a simmer, drop in the dumplings, cover, and cook for 2 minutes if the dumplings are fresh, or 4 minutes if frozen. Fish them out of the soup with a spider skimmer or slotted spoon and divide the soup among four bowls.

• **Make the bowls:** Float 6 dumplings in each soup bowl or divide the salad among four bowls and arrange 6 dumplings on each salad. Serve immediately.

a few tips for streamlining bowls

Component cooking usually entails a few different things happening at the same time, with the expectation that everything is ready and hot for the final moment of assembly. It can seem overwhelming when you're first getting used to it. Here are a few tips for simplifying and streamlining bowls.

USE YOUR MICROWAVE: A microwave comes in very handy for broth dishes in particular, saving space and time. Use it to heat up ramen or pho broth just before serving, rather than using a saucepan. This is also a good way to reheat leftover rice or to warm other leftovers to be repurposed in bowls.

COOK NOODLES AHEAD OF TIME: I had the misconception that dried noodles needed to be cooked fresh to order, unless used in something like a cold noodle salad. On the contrary, after cooking Asian noodles (or any type of noodle or pasta), you can rinse them under cold running water to cool them and remove the starch, drain thoroughly, then portion into resealable bags. These can be stored in the refrigerator for up to 3 days or the freezer for 1 month. To reheat, just drop into a saucepan of boiling water for about 30 seconds for refrigerated noodles or about 1½ minutes for frozen. Taste to make sure they're heated through.

USE A RICE COOKER: This can be an excellent way to simplify, both by eliminating a pan from the stovetop and by reducing the margin of error if you have a history of screwing up stovetop rice. For more on rice cookers, see page 20.

"PREHEAT" YOUR SERVING BOWLS: This may sound like an added step, but one of the challenges of making component-based bowls is making sure everything is hot when you serve them. To help in this regard, pour enough boiling or very hot water into your serving bowls to fill them halfway and let stand for about 10 minutes as you finish preparing your meal, enough time for the bowl to thoroughly heat up. Pour out the water just before assembly.

MAXIMIZE YOUR STACKING STEAMER UNIT: A stacking steamer unit can be used to steam vegetables as well as dumplings. One advantage of having multiple layers is that you can easily steam a few different vegetables all at once—summer squash on one layer and sweet potatoes on another, for example. This is a great way to double down. Use caution when opening it up, as a cloud of steam will billow out.

THINK LIKE A PREP COOK: Prep cooks at restaurants spend their days getting all the various ingredients ready for chefs and line cooks—they prepare meats and vegetables, make condiments and stock, and toast nuts and seeds. Read a recipe over and clean and chop the vegetables, soak the grains or kombu, make the stock, or toast the nuts ahead of time.

KEEP COMPONENTS WARM: As you cook various components one at a time, keep them warm by either covering them with a piece of aluminum foil, or, if they're going to sit for more than a few minutes, covering them with a piece of foil and transferring to an oven or toaster oven preheated to 250°F.

leek shumai

On their own, these dumplings make a great kickoff to a dinner party, with a flavor profile that's amenable to almost anything that's on your menu. They are succulent, savory, and elegant, much more than the sum of the small list of ingredients, with earthy mushrooms, sweet sautéed leeks, a touch of savory roundness from light miso, and a final kick from a good amount of black pepper. Wash the leeks thoroughly to rid them of dirt that gets caught inside: Trim off the root ends, split them in half lengthwise, and peel them open with your fingers under running water, allowing the water to run through the leaves. MAKES 25 TO 30 DUMPLINGS

3 dried shiitake mushrooms

1 cup hot water

1 tablespoon apple cider vinegar or sherry vinegar

1 tablespoon light-colored miso paste

2 tablespoons neutral-tasting oil

2 medium leeks, white and pale green parts only, thoroughly cleaned and thinly sliced

Pinch of fine sea salt

2 teaspoons minced garlic

10 ounces white button or cremini mushrooms, finely chopped

3 tablespoons minced fresh parsley

¼ teaspoon freshly ground black pepper

Pinch of sugar (optional)

25 to 30 thin square dumpling wrappers

for the bowls

Green Salad with Honey-Soy Vinaigrette (page 204) or Toasted Quinoa with Massaged Kale (page 210)

• Place the dried mushrooms in a small bowl and cover with the hot water. Let stand for at least 20 to 30 minutes, until completely tender. Drain, reserving the liquid. Discard the stems and finely chop the caps.

• Measure out ¼ cup of the mushroom soaking liquid into a cup or bowl, pouring carefully so as to leave any grit behind. Discard any soaking liquid that remains, or reserve it for another use. Stir in the vinegar and miso until well combined.

- Heat 1 tablespoon of the oil in a wide skillet over medium heat. Add the leeks and a pinch of salt and cook, stirring periodically, until the leeks are tender and beginning to caramelize, 8 to 10 minutes. Stir in the garlic and once it is fragrant, add half of the reserved miso-mushroom liquid, scraping up any brown bits from the bottom of the pan with a wooden spoon. Continue cooking until the pan is mostly dry, another minute or so. Transfer to a mixing bowl.

- Wipe out the skillet, return it to the heat, and add the remaining 1 tablespoon oil. Add the fresh mushrooms and cook, stirring periodically, until they begin to release some of their liquid, 5 to 7 minutes. Add the reconstituted mushrooms and cook for 3 to 5 minutes more, until the pan is mostly dry. Add the remaining reserved miso-mushroom liquid, scraping up any browned bits from the bottom of the pan with a wooden spoon. Continue cooking until the pan is mostly dry. Stir in the parsley and pepper, then transfer to the mixing bowl with the leeks. Mix to combine, then taste, adding a pinch of salt, pepper, or sugar if needed. Let cool completely.

- Set up your dumpling assembly station: Place a stack of dumpling wrappers on one end of a cutting board and cover with a lightly moistened towel or paper towel to prevent them from drying out. Place a small bowl of water and the prepared filling within reach. Also set out a parchment-lined baking sheet and moistened clean towel, for the assembled dumplings.

- Fill and shape the dumplings into shumai (see page 169), arranging them on the baking sheet as you go and covering with the towel to prevent them from drying out. If you're not eating them immediately, place the tray in the freezer for 30 minutes, until the dumplings have firmed up, then transfer to an airtight container or resealable bag and keep them in the freezer until ready to serve.

- To steam the dumplings, heat about ½ inch of water in a skillet until simmering. Use a paper towel moistened with a bit of oil to lightly grease the layers of a stacking steamer unit, then arrange the fresh or frozen dumplings inside so that they're not touching. Place the steamer in the simmering water. Cook for 3 minutes if the dumplings are fresh, or 5 minutes if frozen. Use caution when opening the steamer, as a cloud of steam will billow out.

- **Make the bowls:** Divide the salad or quinoa among four bowls. Arrange 6 dumplings on top of the salad or quinoa in each bowl and serve immediately.

spicy carrot dumplings

FLAME-ROASTED JALAPEÑO, SCALLIONS, PEANUTS

These dumplings are spicy and a little smoky and have a tender texture. Blistering jalapeño peppers over a gas flame is a quick way to transform them into something new, and since jalapeños can vary a lot in terms of spiciness, it's important to taste as you go (it's easier to add than take away). If you serve the dumplings over salad, garnish liberally with fresh herbs like basil and mint, and sprinkle with chopped roasted peanuts. You can also serve them as a snack or starter drizzled with the peanut dressing from the Gado-Gado recipe on page 64. MAKES 25 TO 30 DUMPLINGS

4 medium carrots (6 to 8 ounces total), sliced into ½-inch-thick rounds

1 jalapeño pepper

2 scallions, green and white parts, thinly sliced

1 teaspoon minced garlic

1 tablespoon olive oil

1 teaspoon lime juice

½ teaspoon fine sea salt

Pinch of sugar

Freshly ground black pepper

3 tablespoons minced fresh cilantro

3 tablespoons chopped roasted peanuts

25 to 30 round or square thin dumpling wrappers

for the bowls

Fragrant Wonton Soup (page 203), Green Salad with Honey-Soy Vinaigrette (page 204), or Toasted Quinoa with Massaged Kale (page 210)

• Bring about an inch of water to boil in a saucepan fitted with a steamer basket. Add the carrots, cover, and steam until completely tender, 5 to 8 minutes. Remove the carrots and let cool.

• Meanwhile, roast the jalapeño directly over the flame of a gas burner, turning it periodically, until blackened and blistered all over, 4 to 7 minutes. You can set a metal cooling rack—one that you don't mind taking on some burn marks—on the burner and then set the jalapeño on it, or you can hold the pepper in the flame with heatproof tongs. (Alternatively, if you don't have a gas range, preheat the broiler to high. Set the jalapeño on a baking sheet or in a skillet and place it close to the heat source. Roast, turning periodically, until blistered all over.)

• Transfer the jalapeño to a bowl and cover tightly with plastic wrap. Let stand for 10 minutes, or until cool enough to handle. Gently rub off the blackened skin. Split the jalapeño lengthwise, trim out the seeds and ribs, and then finely chop. Taste a piece—if it's uncomfortably spicy, start with only half of the jalapeño in the next step, and add more as needed. (Wash your hands immediately after handling the jalapeño.)

• Place the carrots, jalapeño, scallions, garlic, oil, lime juice, salt, sugar, and a few grinds of black pepper in the bowl of a food processor. Pulse until coarsely mashed. Stir in the cilantro and peanuts. (You can also mash carrots in a mixing bowl with a fork—you should have pieces no larger than peas.) Taste for seasoning and add salt, black pepper, lime juice, sugar, or any reserved jalapeño, as needed.

• Set up your dumpling assembly station: Place a stack of dumpling wrappers on one end of a cutting board and cover with a lightly moistened towel or paper towel to prevent them from drying out. Place a small bowl of water and the dumpling filling within reach. Also set out a parchment-lined baking sheet and moistened clean towel for the assembled dumplings.

• Fill and shape the dumplings (see page 168), arranging them on the baking sheet as you go and covering with the towel to prevent them from drying out. If you're not eating them immediately, place the tray in the freezer for 30 minutes, until the dumplings have firmed up, then transfer to an airtight container or resealable bag and keep them in the freezer until ready to serve.

• **To steam the dumplings:** Heat about ½ inch of water in a skillet until simmering. Lightly grease the layers of a stacking steamer unit, then arrange the dumplings inside so that they're not touching. Place the steamer in the simmering water. Cook for 3 minutes if the dumplings are fresh, or 5 minutes if frozen. Use caution when opening the steamer, as a cloud of steam will billow out.

• **To boil the dumplings:** With the soup at a simmer, drop in the dumplings, cover, and cook for 2 minutes if the dumplings are fresh or 4 minutes if frozen. Fish them out of the soup with a spider skimmer or slotted spoon and divide the soup among four bowls.

• **Make the bowls:** Divide the salad or quinoa among four bowls. Arrange 6 dumplings on top of the salad or quinoa in each bowl, or float them in the soup and serve immediately.

napa cabbage and peanut shumai

SHIITAKES, SCALLIONS, TOFU

Cabbage and shiitakes are common in Asian-style filled vegetarian dumplings, as are the soy, garlic, and sesame oil, which makes these dumplings a bit more traditional than others in this chapter. They have a lot of crunchy texture from the peanuts, cabbage, and even the crispy-fried tofu. But don't worry if the filling looks too loose; that texture is important so as to avoid mushiness. Try to get raw peanuts and roast them just before cooking—it greatly amplifies their toasty flavor. I like these best shaped as shumai, but if you want to serve them in the miso soup on page 206, shape them into half moons or triangles. MAKES 25 TO 30 DUMPLINGS

3 dried shiitake mushrooms

4.5 ounces firm tofu (about one-third of a 14-ounce block), blotted dry

1 tablespoon neutral-tasting oil

1½ cups finely shredded cabbage

2 teaspoons minced garlic

1 tablespoon soy sauce

1½ teaspoons rice vinegar

1½ teaspoons brown sugar

¾ teaspoon fine sea salt

1 scant teaspoon toasted sesame oil

3 scallions, white and green parts, thinly sliced

2 tablespoons minced fresh chives

3 tablespoons coarsely chopped peanuts

25 to 30 thin round or square dumpling wrappers

for the bowls

Green Salad with Honey-Soy Vinaigrette (page 204), Stir-Fried Bok Choy and Rice (page 208), or Toasted Quinoa with Massaged Kale (page 210)

• Cover the dried mushrooms with hot water and let stand for 20 to 30 minutes, until completely softened. Drain, reserving the liquid for stock or another use if desired, and gently squeeze the mushrooms dry. Discard the stems and finely chop the caps.

• Put the tofu on a cutting board or in a mixing bowl and coarsely mash it with a fork.

• Heat the neutral-tasting oil in a skillet over medium heat. Add the cabbage and cook, stirring occasionally, until tender and caramelizing a bit, 10 to 15 minutes. Stir in the mashed tofu and cook for another 3 to 5 minutes, until the pan is quite dry. Add the garlic and cook, stirring for 30 seconds or so until fragrant, then add the soy sauce, vinegar, brown sugar, and salt, scraping up any browned bits from the bottom of the pan with a wooden spoon. After 2 or 3 minutes, when the pan seems dry again, remove from the heat. Stir in the chopped mushroom caps, sesame oil, scallions, chives, and peanuts. Let cool completely.

• Set up your dumpling assembly station: Place a stack of dumpling wrappers on one end of a cutting board and cover with a lightly moistened towel or paper towel to prevent them from drying out. Place a small bowl of water and the prepared filling within reach. Also set out a parchment-lined baking sheet and moistened clean towel, for the assembled dumplings.

• Fill and shape the dumplings into shumai (see page 169), arranging them on the baking sheet as you go and covering with the towel to prevent them from drying out. If you're not eating them immediately, place the tray in the freezer for 30 minutes, until the dumplings have firmed up, then transfer to an airtight container or resealable bag and keep them in the freezer until ready to serve.

• To steam the dumplings, heat about ½ inch of water in a skillet until simmering. Use a paper towel moistened with a bit of oil to lightly grease the layers of a stacking steamer unit, then arrange fresh or frozen dumplings inside so that they're not touching. Place the steamer in the simmering water. Cook for 3 minutes if the dumplings are fresh, or 5 minutes if frozen. Use caution when opening the steamer, as a cloud of steam will billow out.

• **Make the bowls:** Divide the salad, bok choy and rice, or quinoa among four bowls. Arrange 6 dumplings on top of the salad or grains in each bowl and serve immediately.

summer squash dumplings

These dumplings are substantial, succulent, and simple. Salting watery vegetables like summer squash improves their structure while also seasoning them. In addition, salting eliminates the necessity of cooking them. Summer squash pairs beautifully with almonds or walnuts and basil or mint, and a bit of Parmesan adds savoriness. I like these best over a salad of crisp mixed greens. Think of the salad as a way to reinforce the flavors in the dumpling filling: Add basil or mint leaves, a handful of toasted nuts, and a dusting of Parmesan cheese. MAKES 25 TO 30 DUMPLINGS

1 medium zucchini or yellow summer squash (about 12 ounces)

1 teaspoon salt

2 tablespoons chopped toasted almonds or walnuts

2 scallions, green and white parts, thinly sliced

3 tablespoons grated Parmesan

3 tablespoons coarsely chopped fresh basil or mint

2 teaspoons olive oil

1 teaspoon minced garlic

¼ teaspoon finely grated lemon zest

½ teaspoon lemon juice

Pinch of red pepper flakes

Freshly ground black pepper

25 to 30 thin round or square dumpling wrappers

for the bowls

Green Salad with Honey-Soy Vinaigrette (page 204) or Toasted Quinoa with Massaged Kale (page 210)

• Grate the squash using the large holes of a box grater. Line a colander with a few layers of cheesecloth. Transfer the grated squash to the colander and toss with the salt. Let stand for 20 minutes, then gather it up in the cheesecloth and wring gently to extract as much liquid as possible.

• Put the squash in a mixing bowl and loosen it up with a fork. Add the nuts along with the scallions, cheese, basil, oil, garlic, lemon zest and juice, red pepper flakes, and a few grinds of black pepper. Taste and adjust the seasoning as necessary.

• Set up your dumpling assembly station: Place a stack of dumpling wrappers on one end of a cutting board and cover with a lightly moistened towel or paper towel to prevent them from drying out. Place a small bowl of water and the dumpling filling within reach. Also set out a parchment-lined baking sheet and moistened clean towel for the assembled dumplings.

• Shape the dumplings into half moons or triangles or nurses' caps (see page 168), arranging them on the baking sheet as you go and covering with the towel to prevent them from drying out. If you're not eating them immediately, place the tray in the freezer for 30 minutes, until the dumplings have firmed up, then transfer to an airtight container or resealable bag and keep them in the freezer until ready to serve.

• To steam the dumplings, heat about ½ inch of water in a skillet until simmering. Use a paper towel moistened with a bit of oil to lightly grease the layers of a stacking steamer unit, then arrange the fresh or frozen dumplings inside so that they're not touching. Place the steamer in the simmering water. Cook for 3 minutes if the dumplings are fresh, or 5 minutes if frozen. Use caution when opening the steamer, as a cloud of steam will billow out.

• **Make the bowls:** Divide the salad or quinoa among four bowls. Arrange 6 dumplings on top of the salad or quinoa in each bowl and serve immediately.

sesame beet dumplings

Beets and tahini are an unexpectedly terrific combination—sweet and earthy, succulent and creamy—with a buttery flavor and texture. You can steam or roast the beets yourself (see note, page 186), which does taste the best, but for this recipe the vacuum pouches of cooked beets sold in the produce section of many grocery stores are a fine second-best option. If you use fresh beets with attractive greens still attached, serve the greens in place of or in addition to the Stir-Fried Bok Choy and Rice, cooking them just until wilted and silky, 2 to 4 minutes. MAKES 25 TO 30 DUMPLINGS

½ cup finely shredded cabbage

½ teaspoon salt

8 ounces cooked beets, grated

1 tablespoon olive oil

½ teaspoon ground cumin

¼ teaspoon freshly ground black pepper

3 tablespoons well-stirred tahini

½ cup minced fresh chives

2 tablespoons toasted sesame seeds

Lemon juice, to taste

Pinch of sugar (optional)

25 to 30 thin round or square dumpling wrappers

for the bowls

Stir-Fried Bok Choy and Rice (page 208), Toasted Quinoa with Massaged Kale (page 210), or Green Salad with Honey-Soy Vinaigrette (page 204)

• Combine the cabbage and salt in a colander. Let stand for 20 minutes, until slightly wilted. Gently squeeze to extract excess moisture.

• Stir together the cabbage, beets, olive oil, cumin, and pepper. Fold in the tahini, chives, sesame seeds, and a squeeze of lemon juice. Taste and add more salt or lemon juice or a pinch of sugar, as needed.

• Set up your dumpling assembly station: Place a stack of dumpling wrappers on one end of

a cutting board and cover with a lightly moistened towel or paper towel to prevent them from drying out. Place a small bowl of water and the dumpling filling within reach. Also set out a parchment-lined baking sheet and a moistened clean towel for the assembled dumplings.

• Shape the dumplings into half moons or triangles or nurses' caps (see page 168), arranging them on the baking sheet as you go and covering with the towel to prevent them from drying out. If you're not eating them immediately, place the tray in the freezer for 30 minutes, until the dumplings have firmed up, then transfer to an airtight container or resealable bag and keep them in the freezer until ready to serve.

• To steam the dumplings, heat about ½ inch of water in a skillet until simmering. Use a paper towel moistened with a bit of oil to lightly grease the layers of a stacking steamer unit, then arrange the fresh or frozen dumplings inside so that they're not touching. Place the steamer in the simmering water. Cook for 3 minutes if the dumplings are fresh, or 5 minutes if frozen. Use caution when opening the steamer, as a cloud of steam will billow out.

• **Make the bowls:** Divide the bok choy and rice, quinoa, or salad among four bowls. Arrange 6 dumplings on top of the salad or grains in each bowl and serve immediately.

roasting beets

Roasting beets only requires heat and patience. Cooking times tend to vary a lot, so the most important thing is to not remove them from the oven too soon.

Preheat your oven to 375°F. Scrub the beets clean and trim the ends. Arrange in a single, snug layer in a casserole or other baking pan. Drizzle with olive oil and use your hands to thoroughly coat them. Add about ⅛ inch water to the bottom of the pan. Cover tightly with foil and roast for 30 to 90 minutes, checking first after 30 minutes and then every 15 to 30 minutes as necessary, until the beets can be easily pierced with a skewer or a narrow, sharp knife. Cool until safe to handle. While the beets are still warm, the skins usually rub right off.

savory fall dumplings

Brussels sprouts, with their pleasant crunchy-chewy quality (when not cooked to mush, of course), have a texture that's perfectly suited to dumplings. Caramelized onions complement their flavor, and cooked egg—in this case, essentially a Chinese egg crepe that's shredded up and stirred into the filling—adds some protein, moisture, and richness. To make these vegan, simply swap out the egg for 3 tablespoons of firm tofu that's been mashed up with a fork, and adjust the seasoning as needed before you proceed with shaping the dumplings. MAKES 25 TO 30 DUMPLINGS

8 ounces small, firm Brussels sprouts (scant 2 cups)

2 tablespoons plus 1 teaspoon neutral-tasting oil

1 small onion, diced

½ teaspoon fine sea salt

2 teaspoons minced garlic

2 tablespoons apple cider vinegar

1 tablespoon water

1 egg

Freshly ground black pepper

25 to 30 round thick or thin dumpling wrappers

for the bowls

Stir-Fried Bok Choy and Rice (page 208) or Toasted Quinoa with Massaged Kale (page 210)

• Trim the root ends off the Brussels sprouts and remove any discolored outer leaves. Cut each head in half lengthwise, through the stem. Place the flat side down on the cutting board and julienne the halves into thin strips. (Alternatively, slice them by sending the whole sprouts through the slicing blade of a food processor.)

• Heat 2 tablespoons of the oil in a medium skillet over medium-low heat. Add the onion and salt and cook, stirring frequently, for 15 to 20 minutes, until the onion is golden and caramelized. Raise the heat slightly and stir in the Brussels sprouts. Cook for 5 to 7 minutes, until the Brussels sprouts are just tender. Stir in the garlic, then add the vinegar and the water and use a wooden spoon to scrape up the browned bits from the bottom of the pan. Transfer the Brussels sprouts to a mixing bowl to cool.

• Meanwhile, crack the egg into a small bowl. Add a pinch of salt and whisk thoroughly, until frothy. Heat the remaining 1 teaspoon oil in a small skillet over medium heat. Once hot, pour in the egg. The idea is to make a thin pancake: Tuck a rubber spatula under one cooked edge of the egg, tilt the pan, and allow the uncooked egg to run underneath. Then tuck the spatula under the opposite cooked edge, gently grab the egg with your fingers, and flip it over. The whole process will only take around 90 seconds, and don't fret if the pancake tears, since you will be chopping it. (You can also just scramble the egg.) Transfer to a plate or cutting board to cool, then roughly chop into small pieces and stir into the Brussels sprouts filling.

• Stir in several grinds of black pepper into the dumpling filling. Taste, and add another pinch of salt if needed. Make sure the filling is completely cool before proceeding.

• Set up your dumpling assembly station: Place a stack of dumpling wrappers on one end of a cutting board and cover with a lightly moistened towel or paper towel to prevent them from drying out. Place a small bowl of water and the dumpling filling within reach. Also set out a parchment-lined baking sheet and moistened clean towel for the assembled dumplings.

• Shape the dumplings into half moons or triangles, nurses' caps, or bunched wontons (see page 168), arranging them on the baking sheet as you go and covering with the towel to prevent them from drying out. If you're not eating them immediately, place the tray in the freezer for 30 minutes, until the dumplings have firmed up, then transfer to an airtight container or resealable bag and keep them in the freezer until ready to serve.

• To steam the dumplings, heat about ½ inch of water in a skillet until simmering. Use a paper towel moistened with a bit of oil to lightly grease the layers of a stacking steamer unit, then arrange the fresh or frozen dumplings inside so that they're not touching. Place the steamer in the simmering water. Cook for 3 minutes if the dumplings are fresh, or 5 minutes if frozen. Use caution when opening the steamer, as a cloud of steam will billow out.

• **Make the bowls:** Divide the bok choy and rice or quinoa among four bowls. Arrange 6 dumplings on top of the grains in each bowl and serve immediately.

kimchi dumplings

RIPE KIMCHI, TOFU, SCALLIONS

Korean steamed, pan-fried, or sometimes deep-fried dumplings are called *mandu*, and this recipe is my version of a vegetarian, kimchi-based one. The more ripened your kimchi, the more flavor it will contribute to the dumplings. The brine is used as an ingredient, too—it's very flavorful and can function like vinegar in your cooking, so you definitely don't want to waste it. I like these shaped into potstickers and pan-fried, as instructed below. I always serve them with a little pile of kimchi and some other crunchy vegetables as garnishes—radishes or daikon, carrots, and cucumbers, which can be salted and tossed in a little rice vinegar—and with Gochujang Sauce for drizzling. MAKES 25 TO 30 DUMPLINGS

7 ounces firm tofu (half of a 14-ounce block), pressed (see page 119)

1 cup Napa Cabbage or Bok Choy Kimchi, preferably homemade (see page 227)

3 tablespoons neutral-tasting oil

1 teaspoon sugar

Kimchi brine or rice vinegar, as needed

2 tablespoons soy sauce

3 scallions, green and white parts, thinly sliced

25 to 30 thick round dumpling wrappers

for the bowls

Stir-Fried Bok Choy and Rice (page 208)

Gochujang Sauce (page 242), for serving

• Place the tofu in the middle of a cutting board and mash it up with a fork.

• After measuring the kimchi, hold it in place in the measuring cup, turn the cup upside down over a small bowl, and press to extract the kimchi brine, draining it into the bowl; set the brine aside. Finely chop the kimchi.

• Heat 1 tablespoon of the oil in a wide skillet over medium-high heat. Add the tofu and cook, stirring periodically, for 5 to 7 minutes, until beginning to get crispy and golden brown. Add the kimchi and sugar and cook for another 3 to 5 minutes, until the kimchi is softened and the pan is dry. Pour in 3 tablespoons of the reserved kimchi brine (if there's not enough brine, use either additional kimchi brine from the jar or rice vinegar to make up the volume) and the soy sauce, scraping up any browned bits from the pan with a wooden spoon. When the pan is dry again, remove from the heat and stir in the scallions. Let cool completely.

• Set up your dumpling assembly station: Place a stack of dumpling wrappers on one end of a cutting board and cover with a lightly moistened towel or paper towel to prevent them from drying out. Place a small bowl of water and the dumpling filling within reach. Also set out a parchment-lined baking sheet and moistened clean towel for the assembled dumplings.

• Shape the dumplings into pleated potstickers (see page 169), arranging them on the baking sheet as you go and covering with a towel to prevent them from drying out. If you're not eating them immediately, place the tray in the freezer for 30 minutes, until the dumplings have firmed up, then transfer to an airtight container or resealable bag and keep them in the freezer until ready to serve.

• To cook, heat a heavy skillet over medium-high heat. Swirl in the remaining 2 tablespoons oil. Once hot, arrange the dumplings in concentric circles in the pan, flat side down, fitting as many as you can into the pan in a single layer. Cook for 2 to 3 minutes if freshly made or 4 to 6 minutes if frozen, until golden brown on the bottoms and crisp. (Use your fingers to lift one out of the pan to check.) Working quickly, drizzle with about 3 tablespoons water and then cover the pan tightly with a lid or piece of foil. Cook for 3 minutes more, until the dumplings appear translucent and are heated through.

• **Make the bowls:** Divide the bok choy and rice among four bowls. Arrange 6 potstickers on top of the bok choy and rice in each bowl and serve immediately with the Gochujang Sauce.

parsnip dumplings

Almonds bridge the flavors of carrots and parsnips in these dumplings. (This filling is terrific on its own—it makes a great salad addition to a mezze platter.) You can substitute well-toasted sunflower seeds, which lack the sweetness of almonds but add a pleasant nutty flavor. The best parsnips are available in the late fall or early winter—they're a cold weather vegetable that, like cabbage, benefit from a crop freeze, which crystallizes the sugars and makes them sweeter. If your parsnips are especially thick, halve them lengthwise and trim out the core, which can be very tough and fibrous. MAKES 25 TO 30 DUMPLINGS

2 tablespoons neutral-tasting oil

1 cup shredded carrots (from about 2 medium, 5 ounces)

1 cup shredded parsnips (from 2 to 3 medium, 5 ounces)

½ teaspoon salt

Pinch of red pepper flakes

2 teaspoons minced garlic

2 scallions, white and green parts, thinly sliced

2 tablespoons apple cider vinegar

½ cup minced fresh cilantro

⅓ cup finely chopped roasted almonds

Freshly ground black pepper

25 to 30 thin round or square dumpling wrappers

for the bowls

Fragrant Wonton Soup (page 203), Green Salad with Honey-Soy Vinaigrette (page 204), or Toasted Quinoa with Massaged Kale (page 210)

• Heat the oil in a wide skillet over medium heat. Add the carrots, parsnips, salt, and red pepper flakes. Cook, tossing frequently with tongs, until mostly soft and beginning to caramelize, 6 to 10 minutes. Stir in the garlic and scallions and cook for about 1 minute more, until fragrant, then add the vinegar, scraping up any browned bits from the pan with a wooden spoon, and cook for 1 to 2 minutes more, stirring constantly, until the pan is dry. Let cool completely. Fold in the cilantro and almonds and add a few grinds of black pepper. Taste, adding more salt or a splash of vinegar as needed.

• Set up your dumpling assembly station: Place a stack of dumpling wrappers on one end of a cutting board and cover with a lightly moistened towel or paper towel to prevent them from drying out. Place a small bowl of water and the dumpling filling within reach. Also set out a parchment-lined baking sheet and a moistened clean towel for the assembled dumplings.

• Shape the dumplings into half moons or triangles or nurses' caps (see page 168), arranging them on the baking sheet as you go and covering with the towel to prevent them from drying out. If you're not eating them immediately, place the tray in the freezer for 30 minutes, until the dumplings have firmed up, then transfer to an airtight container or resealable bag and keep them in the freezer until ready to serve.

• **To steam the dumplings:** Heat about ½ inch of water in a skillet until simmering. Use a paper towel moistened with a bit of oil to lightly grease the layers of a stacking steamer unit, then arrange fresh or frozen dumplings inside so that they're not touching. Place the steamer in the simmering water. Cook for 3 minutes if the dumplings are fresh, or 5 minutes if frozen. Use caution when opening the steamer, as a cloud of steam will billow out.

• **To boil the dumplings:** With the soup at a simmer, drop in the dumplings, cover, and cook for 2 minutes if the dumplings are fresh, or 4 minutes if frozen. Fish them out of the soup with a spider skimmer or slotted spoon and divide the soup among four bowls.

• **For the bowls:** Divide the salad or quinoa among four bowls. Arrange 6 dumplings on top of the salad or quinoa in each bowl or float them in the soup and serve immediately.

chickpea potstickers

I like these dumplings best as potstickers because the sturdy, savory filling is completely addictive against the crisp, golden crust that develops in pan-frying. Quick-pickled shallots add further contrast in the form of bursts of sweet, sharp crunch. I recommend doing all of the chopping by hand rather than using a food processor in this recipe—it's important that the filling have lots of texture, and with a food processor, it's too easy to turn it into a hummus-like mush. MAKES 25 TO 30 DUMPLINGS

2 tablespoons red wine vinegar

1½ teaspoons sugar

1 teaspoon fine sea salt

1 shallot, diced

6 ounces kale (1 small or ½ large bunch), coarsely chopped, stems and all

1 cup cooked chickpeas (rinsed if canned)

1 tablespoon olive oil

1 garlic clove, smashed and coarsely chopped

¾ teaspoon ground cumin

½ teaspoon smoked paprika

¼ teaspoon freshly ground black pepper

25 to 30 thick round dumpling wrappers

2 tablespoons neutral-tasting oil

for the bowls

Green Salad with Honey-Soy Vinaigrette (page 204), Toasted Quinoa with Massaged Kale (page 210), or Stir-Fried Bok Choy and Rice (page 208)

• Whisk together the vinegar, sugar, and ½ teaspoon salt in a bowl until the sugar and salt dissolve. Add the shallot and let stand for at least 20 minutes, as you prepare the rest of the filling, stirring periodically.

• Meanwhile, bring a saucepan of water to boil and salt it generously. Prepare an ice-water bath. Add the kale to the saucepan and blanch for 2 to 5 minutes, until the stems are tender. Drain the kale and add it to the ice-water bath. Drain again and squeeze out excess moisture, then finely chop the kale.

• Place the chickpeas in a mixing bowl and mash coarsely with a potato masher or fork. Add the kale, olive oil, garlic, cumin, paprika, pepper, and the remaining ½ teaspoon salt. Lift the shallots from the vinegar with a slotted spoon and add them, as well as 1 tablespoon of the pickling brine. Stir to combine. Taste, adding additional salt or a bit more of the pickling vinegar to brighten the flavor if necessary.

• Set up your dumpling assembly station: Place a stack of dumpling wrappers on one end of a cutting board and cover with a lightly moistened towel or paper towel to prevent them from drying out. Place a small bowl of water and the prepared filling within reach. Also set out a parchment-lined baking sheet and a moistened clean towel, for the assembled dumplings.

• Fill and shape the dumplings into pleated potstickers (see page 169) arranging them on the baking sheet as you go and covering with the towel to prevent them from drying out. If you're not eating them immediately, place the tray in the freezer for 30 minutes, until the dumplings are firmed up, then transfer to an airtight container or resealable bag and keep them in the freezer until ready to serve.

• To cook, heat a heavy skillet over medium-high heat. Swirl in the neutral-tasting oil. Once hot, arrange the dumplings in concentric circles in the pan, flat side down, fitting as many as you can into the pan in a single layer. Cook for 2 to 3 minutes if the dumplings are fresh, or 4 to 6 minutes if frozen, until golden brown on the bottoms and crisp. (Use your fingers to lift one out of the pan to check.) Working quickly, drizzle with about 3 tablespoons water and then cover the pan tightly with a lid or piece of foil. Cook for 3 minutes more, until the dumplings appear translucent and are heated through.

• **Make the bowls:** Divide the salad, quinoa, or bok choy and rice among four bowls. Arrange 6 potstickers on top of the salad or grains in each bowl and serve immediately.

kabocha dumplings

Kabocha squash is sometimes marked "Japanese pumpkin" at markets and Asian grocery stores. Its skin features streaks of dark green and orange, and the flesh has a vibrant reddish hue and a sharp fruity fragrance, and it is a bit starchier than pumpkin and butternut squash once cooked. Here it's simply grated and sautéed, then paired with flavors that highlight its sweet, autumnal notes: fennel, ginger, coconut milk, and a pinch of cayenne for heat. MAKES 25 TO 30 DUMPLINGS

1 tablespoon neutral-tasting oil

½ medium onion, diced

2½ cups grated kabocha squash (about 1 pound seeded squash)

½ teaspoon fennel seeds, crushed

½ teaspoon sugar

¼ teaspoon fine sea salt

Pinch of cayenne pepper

1 tablespoon minced garlic

1 tablespoon grated fresh ginger

½ cup coconut milk

¼ cup coarsely chopped fresh cilantro

1 teaspoon grated orange zest

25 to 30 thin round or square dumpling wrappers

for the bowls

Green Salad with Honey-Soy Vinaigrette (page 204) or Toasted Quinoa with Massaged Kale (page 210)

• Heat the oil in a skillet over medium heat. Add the onion and cook, stirring periodically, until translucent, 3 to 5 minutes. Add the squash, fennel seeds, sugar, salt, and cayenne and turn up the heat to medium-high. Cook until the squash is soft and blistered in parts, stirring occasionally, another 3 to 5 minutes. Stir in the garlic and ginger, then the coconut milk. Stir constantly to prevent scorching and cook until the pan is dry, another 2 to 3 minutes. Remove from the heat and let cool completely. Stir in the cilantro and orange zest.

• Set up your dumpling assembly station: Place a stack of dumpling wrappers on one end of a cutting board and cover with a lightly moistened towel or paper towel to prevent them from drying out. Place a small bowl of water and the dumpling filling within reach. Also set out a parchment-lined baking sheet and a moistened clean towel for the assembled dumplings.

• Shape the dumplings into half moons or triangles or nurses' caps (see page 168). If you're not eating them immediately, place the tray in the freezer for 30 minutes, until the dumplings are firmed up, then transfer to an airtight container or resealable bag and keep them in the freezer until ready to serve.

• To steam the dumplings, heat about ½ inch of water in a skillet until simmering. Use a paper towel moistened with a bit of oil to lightly grease the layers of a stacking steamer unit, then arrange the fresh or frozen dumplings inside so that they're not touching. Place the steamer in the simmering water. Cook for 3 minutes if the dumplings are fresh, or 5 minutes if frozen. Use caution when opening the steamer, as a cloud of steam will billow out.

• **Make the bowls:** Divide the salad or quinoa among four bowls. Arrange 6 dumplings on top of the salad or quinoa in each bowl and serve immediately.

rich lentil dumplings

The flavor profile of these dumplings is similar to that of a lentil-based pâté, with a foundation of rich and hearty ingredients like lentils, nuts, miso, and caramelized onions. The secret ingredient is *umeboshi* paste, a Japanese pantry staple that's made from coarsely pureed salt-pickled plums. Health food stores often carry it, next to the other Japanese pantry staples. It's a terrific ingredient to keep on hand for dips, dressings, and marinades—whenever you want to add something a little sour, salty, and completely unexpected. MAKES 25 TO 30 DUMPLINGS

½ cup green lentils, rinsed and picked through

½ teaspoon fine sea salt

4 dried shiitake mushrooms

½ cup mung bean sprouts

1 tablespoon light-colored miso paste

1 teaspoon umeboshi paste

1 scallion, white and green parts, thinly sliced

¼ cup coarsely chopped fresh cilantro leaves and stems

3 tablespoons finely chopped toasted walnuts

¼ teaspoon freshly ground black pepper

25 to 30 thin or thick square or round dumpling wrappers

2 tablespoons neutral-tasting oil, if pan-frying

for the bowls

Stir-Fried Bok Choy and Rice (page 208) or Mushroom Miso Soup with Greens (page 206)

• In a saucepan, cover the lentils with cold water and place over medium-high heat. Bring to a boil, then add the salt, reduce the heat to low, and simmer for about 10 minutes. Taste for doneness—they'll likely need another few minutes, but remove them from the heat before they get mushy. Drain and let cool completely.

• Meanwhile, place the dried mushrooms in a heatproof bowl and cover with hot water. Let stand for 20 to 30 minutes, until the mushrooms are completely tender. Remove from the water and gently squeeze to remove excess liquid. Discard the stems and then finely chop the mushroom caps.

- Place the bean sprouts in a heatproof bowl and cover with boiling water. Immediately drain and rinse under running cold water. Drain thoroughly, then coarsely chop.

- Place the cooked lentils, miso, and *umeboshi* paste in a mixing bowl and use a fork to mash into a chunky paste. Add the mushrooms, bean sprouts, scallion, cilantro, walnuts, and pepper, stirring with the fork until well combined.

- Set up your dumpling assembly station: Place a stack of dumpling wrappers on one end of a cutting board and cover with a lightly moistened towel or paper towel to prevent them from drying out. Place a small bowl of water and the dumpling filling within reach. Also set out a parchment-lined baking sheet and moistened clean towel for the assembled dumplings.

- Shape the dumplings into half moons or triangles, nurses' caps, or, if using thicker dumpling wrappers, pleated potstickers (see page 168), arranging them on the baking sheet as you go and covering with the towel to prevent them from drying out. If you're not eating them immediately, place the tray in the freezer for 30 minutes, until the dumplings have firmed up, then transfer to an airtight container or resealable bag and keep them in the freezer until ready to serve.

- **To steam the dumplings (if using thin dumpling wrappers):** Heat about ½ inch of water in a skillet until simmering. Use a paper towel moistened with oil to lightly grease the layers of a stacking steamer unit, then arrange the dumplings inside so that they're not touching. Place the steamer in the simmering water. Cook for 3 minutes if the dumplings are fresh, or 5 minutes if frozen. Use caution when opening the steamer, as a cloud of steam will billow out.

- **To pan-fry them (if using thick dumpling wrappers):** Heat a heavy skillet over medium-high heat. Swirl in the oil. Once hot, arrange the dumplings in concentric circles in the pan, flat side down, fitting as many as you can into the pan in a single layer. Cook for 2 to 3 minutes if fresh, or 4 to 6 minutes if frozen, until golden brown on the bottoms and crisp. (Use your fingers to lift one out of the pan to check.) Working quickly, drizzle with about 3 tablespoons water and then cover the pan tightly with a lid or piece of foil. Cook for 3 minutes more, until the dumplings appear translucent and are heated through.

- **Make the bowls:** Divide the bok choy and rice or soup among four bowls. Arrange 6 dumplings on top of the bok choy and rice in each bowl or float them in the broth and serve.

sweet potato dumplings

SPINACH, FERMENTED BLACK BEANS, SESAME

Fermented black beans have a salty, umami savoriness that can sometimes be hard to achieve in vegetarian dishes. Called *douchi*, and a fixture of Sichuanese cooking, they're not black beans as we know them from Mexican and Cuban cuisines, but soybeans that have been salted and fermented, so they turn black in the process. They need to be soaked and rinsed before using in order to draw out the salt and mellow the flavor a bit. The best places to find them are at Chinese groceries and online—they should be plump and soft, not completely shriveled and hard. I love them with sweet potatoes and spinach, where they balance out the sweetness with assertive, salty chew. For another use, see the recipe for Chili-Bean Oil on page page 240. MAKES 25 TO 30 DUMPLINGS

3 tablespoons fermented black beans

2 tablespoons neutral-tasting oil

5 ounces spinach (tough stems removed if using mature spinach)

1 tablespoon toasted sesame oil

½ white or red onion, minced

1 small sweet potato or yam (8 ounces), grated

¼ teaspoon fine sea salt

¼ teaspoon sugar

2 teaspoons soy sauce

25 to 30 thin round or square dumpling wrappers

for the bowls

Mushroom Miso Soup with Greens (page 206), Fragrant Wonton Soup (page 203), or Stir-Fried Bok Choy and Rice (page 208)

• Cover the black beans with cold water and let stand while you prepare the rest of the dumpling filling.

• Heat 1 tablespoon neutral-tasting oil in a skillet over medium heat. Add the spinach and cook, tossing with tongs, until wilted, about 2 minutes. Transfer to a cutting board or plate to cool until comfortable to handle. Gently squeeze on the greens to extract as much liquid as possible and pour it off, then finely chop.

• Heat the remaining 1 tablespoon neutral-tasting oil and the sesame oil in a skillet over medium heat. Add the onion and cook, stirring periodically, until softened and beginning to brown, about 10 minutes. Add the sweet potato, salt, and sugar, and cook, stirring periodically, until the sweet potato is tender, another 10 to 15 minutes, then stir in the spinach and soy sauce. Drain the black beans and stir them into the filling. Cook until the pan is dry, then remove from the heat and let cool completely.

• Set up your dumpling assembly station: Place a stack of dumpling wrappers on one end of a cutting board and cover with a lightly moistened towel or paper towel to prevent them from drying out. Place a small bowl of water and the dumpling filling within reach. Also set out a parchment-lined baking sheet and moistened clean towel for the assembled dumplings.

• Shape the dumpling into half moons or triangles, nurses' caps, or bunched wontons (see page 168), arranging them on the baking sheet as you go and covering with the towel to prevent them from drying out. If you're not eating them immediately, place the tray in the freezer for 30 minutes, until the dumplings have firmed up, then transfer to an airtight container or resealable bag and keep them in the freezer until ready to serve.

• **To steam the dumplings:** Heat about ½ inch of water in a skillet until simmering. Use a paper towel moistened with a bit of oil to lightly grease the layers of a stacking steamer unit, then arrange fresh or frozen dumplings inside so that they're not touching. Place the steamer in the simmering water. Cook for 3 minutes if the dumplings are fresh, or 5 minutes if frozen. Use caution when opening the steamer, as a cloud of steam will billow out.

• **To boil the dumplings:** With the soup at a simmer, drop in the dumplings, cover, and cook for 2 minutes if the dumplings are fresh, or 4 minutes if frozen. Fish them out of the soup with a spider skimmer or slotted spoon and divide among the bowls.

• **Make the bowls:** Divide the bok choy and rice among four bowls. Arrange 6 dumplings on top of the bok choy and rice in each bowl or float them in the soup and serve immediately.

bowls for dumplings

fragrant wonton soup

When serving dumplings with soup, you can eliminate a pot from the stove by cooking them in the simmering broth, as instructed here. This simple, aromatic soup is perfect for most of the dumplings in this chapter—its flavor profile is neutral—and it comes together in about 20 minutes. To bulk it up, put a scoop of fresh or leftover rice in the bottom of each bowl. Homemade vegetable stock is ideal here, but a low-salt store-bought one works in a pinch. SERVES 4

1 tablespoon neutral-tasting oil

1 small onion, sliced into thin strips

1 stalk celery, thinly sliced on the bias

1 medium carrot, sliced into thin rounds on the bias

Pinch of red pepper flakes

3 garlic cloves, thinly sliced

2 teaspoons grated fresh ginger

6 cups vegetable stock, preferably homemade (see page 219)

1 teaspoon fine sea salt

4 heads baby bok choy, quartered lengthwise through the core

24 assembled dumplings, fresh or frozen

¼ cup minced fresh chives

2 scallions, white and green parts, thinly sliced

Soy sauce for serving (optional)

Drops of toasted sesame oil for serving (optional)

Rayu (page 238), Chili Oil (page 237), or Chili-Bean Oil (page 240) for serving (optional)

Pounded Ginger Pulp (page 247) for serving (optional)

• Heat the oil in a pot or saucepan over medium heat. Add the onion, celery, carrot, and red pepper flakes. Cook, stirring periodically, for about 5 minutes, until the vegetables are just softened. Stir in the garlic and ginger and cook for 1 minute more, until fragrant. Pour in the stock, bring to a boil, then reduce the heat and simmer for 15 minutes. Add the salt and taste, adding more salt as needed. Add the bok choy and simmer for another 4 to 6 minutes, until tender, then fish out the bok choy with a spider skimmer to prevent overcooking and divide among four bowls.

• Cook the dumplings as directed in the individual recipes.

• Divide the soup among the bowls, float 6 dumplings in each bowl of soup, and serve immediately with chives, scallions, and the condiments of your choice.

green salad with honey-soy vinaigrette

A dumpling salad bowl is the most refreshing way to make a meal out of your homemade dumplings. The Honey-Soy Vinaigrette is a favorite salad dressing of mine, and I'll sometimes use it as a dipping sauce or drizzle when serving dumplings on their own. I've also listed several different toppings that will add different sorts of contrast—juiciness, crunch, and richness. SERVES 4

for the honey-soy vinaigrette

2 tablespoons soy sauce

2 tablespoons brown rice vinegar

1 tablespoon honey

¼ cup neutral-tasting oil

for the salad

24 assembled dumplings, fresh or frozen

8 cups loosely packed tender salad greens

Toppings of choice (below)

Freshly ground black pepper

optional toppings

Citrus: orange, grapefruit, or blood orange segments

Sliced or diced ripe stone fruit: peaches, nectarines, plums, or apricots

Sliced or diced crisp apple or pear

Toasted or roasted nuts or seeds: peanuts, almonds, cashews, walnuts, sunflower seeds, pumpkin seeds

Tamari Sunflower Seeds (recipe follows)

Cold, sliced roasted beets (see page 186)

Avocado chunks

Sliced or diced bell peppers

Diced hard-boiled egg

Sprouts, shoots, or microgreens

Togarashi Blend (page 245)

Frizzled Shallots (page 244)

Garlic Chips (page 243)

Coarsely chopped Napa Cabbage or Bok Choy Kimchi (page 227)

Pickled Red Onions (page 230)

Quick Cucumber Pickles (page 231)

● **Make the dressing:** Whisk together the soy sauce, vinegar, and honey, then pour in the oil in a steady stream while whisking, until emulsified.

- **Make the salad:** Cook the dumplings as directed in the individual recipes.

- Divide the salad greens among four bowls. Arrange 6 hot dumplings over each salad, then add toppings as desired. Just before serving, drizzle the salad with the vinaigrette, about 1½ tablespoons per bowl, and finish with a few grinds of black pepper.

tamari sunflower seeds

Tamari almonds are one of my favorite snacks and salad toppings, but sunflower seeds are a great nut-free option. They're an easy way to add savory toastiness to a dish. MAKES 2 CUPS

2 cups raw, hulled sunflower seeds

½ teaspoon sugar

3 tablespoons tamari or soy sauce

- Preheat the oven to 325°F.

- Spread the sunflower seeds out on a baking sheet. Transfer to the oven and bake, stirring every 10 minutes, until fragrant and beginning to turn golden brown, 20 to 25 minutes. Remove from the oven, sprinkle with the sugar, then pour the tamari over the seeds. Stir quickly so that the seeds are coated evenly. Return the pan to the oven and bake for 8 to 10 minutes more, until the seeds are dry. Let cool completely. Stored in an airtight container, the seeds will keep for 1 week.

mushroom miso soup with greens

Miso soup is a restorative thing on its own, and this recipe is hearty enough to serve without dumplings. The darker your miso paste, the saltier and more assertive the broth will be, so use less to start if you're using a dark brown or red variety and then add more by the teaspoon until it's to your liking. (And if you have a few different kinds of miso paste on hand, try combining them for a more complex flavor.) You can make the broth up to a day or two in advance, then reheat it just before serving as you cook the dumplings—which, if you get in the habit of keeping a stash of dumplings in the freezer, lays the groundwork for a very easy, extra-nourishing weeknight meal. SERVES 4

6 cups water or vegetable stock (preferably homemade, see page 219)

Two 2-inch squares kombu

6 dried shiitake mushrooms

2 tablespoons light-colored miso paste

1 tablespoon soy sauce

1 teaspoon sugar

½ teaspoon fine sea salt

5 ounces firm tofu (about one-third of a 14-ounce package), cubed

¼ cup wakame

4 cups watercress sprigs or baby spinach

24 assembled dumplings, fresh or frozen

2 scallions, white and green parts, thinly sliced on the bias, for garnish

• Heat the water or stock in a pot or saucepan until it just comes to a boil. Remove from the heat and add the kombu and mushrooms. Cover with a lid or plate to trap the steam and let stand for 30 minutes. Strain the broth and return it to the pot. Discard the kombu. Trim off and discard the mushroom stems and thinly slice the caps.

• In a small bowl, whisk together the miso with a ladleful or two of the broth until smooth, then stir the miso mixture into the remaining broth in the pot.

• Just before serving, bring the broth to a simmer and add the soy sauce, sugar, and salt. Taste, adding more miso, salt, or soy sauce as needed. Stir in the mushrooms and tofu.

• At the same time, cover the wakame with cold water in a bowl and let stand for 5 minutes. Drain, squeezing dry, then, if you purchased whole-leaf wakame, coarsely chop it into bite-sized pieces if necessary. Add to the soup.

• Divide the watercress or spinach among four bowls. Cook the dumplings according to the instructions in the individual recipes, then place 6 dumplings on top of the greens in each bowl. Cover with the simmering broth, garnish with the scallions, and serve immediately.

stir-fried bok choy and rice

Here's an easy method for stir-frying bok choy, complete with a flavorful sweet-savory glaze. Baby bok choy is increasingly available outside Asian markets, and I prefer it to the heavier, Napa cabbage–like mature heads. It's light and small—one head fits in the palm of your hand—and is a little sweeter with a more tender texture. I've included instructions here for both the baby and mature vegetable. Rice, greens, dumplings, and a drizzle of the glaze make for a filling bowl meal here, but you might want to add a little garnish of sliced cucumbers or radishes, quick-pickled or raw (see page 231 for Quick Cucumber Pickles), or shredded romaine, butter leaf lettuce, or cabbage for some coolness and extra crunch. SERVES 4

2 pounds bok choy (4 to 6 heads baby bok choy or 1 medium mature head)

4 scallions, white and green parts, trimmed

2 tablespoons plus 2 teaspoons soy sauce, plus more for serving

¼ cup water

2 teaspoons cornstarch or arrowroot powder

2 teaspoons minced garlic

2 teaspoons grated ginger

2 scant teaspoons toasted sesame oil

2 teaspoons brown sugar

Pinch of red pepper flakes

2 tablespoons neutral-tasting oil

5 cups freshly cooked rice or mixed grains (see pages 221–223)

24 assembled dumplings, fresh or frozen

Chili Oil (page 237), for serving (optional)

• If using baby bok choy, quarter the heads lengthwise through the stem. If using mature bok choy, separate the leaves from the stalks. Cut the stalks into 1½-inch segments and chop the leaves in half lengthwise.

• Cut the scallions into 2-inch lengths. If they're thicker than a pencil, slice them in half lengthwise.

• Whisk together the soy sauce, water, cornstarch, garlic, ginger, sesame oil, brown sugar, and red pepper flakes until smooth and the cornstarch is dissolved.

• Heat a wide skillet over medium-high heat and pour in the neutral-tasting oil. Depending on the size of your pan, it may be necessary to cook the bok choy in two batches, in which case, add the soy sauce mixture half at a time in the step below.

• If using baby bok choy, once the oil is shimmering, add the bok choy all at once and cook, stirring frequently, until softened and beginning to brown, 2 to 4 minutes. Add the scallions and cook about 2 minutes more, until limp.

• If using mature bok choy, once the oil is shimmering, add the stems. Cook for about 5 minutes, tossing them periodically, until fork-tender. Stir in the scallions and cook for about 2 minutes, until just limp, then stir in the bok choy leaves.

• Clear away a small space in the center of the pan and pour the soy sauce mixture directly into it (this allows the sauce to caramelize a bit; see note above if you need to cook the bok choy in 2 batches). Stir the vegetables into the liquid and cook for another 1 to 3 minutes, until the sauce thickens. Remove from the heat.

• Cook the dumplings as directed in the individual recipes.

• Divide the rice among four bowls. Use tongs to pile the bok choy on one side of the rice, and arrange 6 dumplings on the other side of each bowl. Drizzle any sauce that remains in the skillet over each serving and serve with additional soy sauce or the Chili Oil, if desired.

toasted quinoa with massaged kale

Ideal for dumplings with unorthodox, non-Asian flavor profiles like Edamame Dumplings (page 170) and Leek Shumai (page 174), this dish is also great for quick, throw-it-together meals and packed lunches on the go. I first learned about toasting quinoa in Marie Simmons's book *Fresh & Fast Vegetarian*. The resulting grains are fluffy and flavorful. And the kale—perked up with garlic and ginger and then a final squeeze of lemon—is another quick recipe that keeps well for a few days. I use it as a condiment on sandwiches and veggie burgers, and on its own. SERVES 4

3 tablespoons olive oil

1½ cups quinoa, rinsed and drained

2½ cups water

1 large bunch lacinato (Tuscan) kale (about 12 ounces)

2 teaspoons grated fresh ginger

1 teaspoon minced garlic

1 teaspoon fine sea salt

24 assembled dumplings, fresh or frozen

½ cup loosely packed mixed fresh herbs or greens, such as parsley, cilantro, chives, dill, basil, mint, carrot or radish tops, and/or tender baby salad greens, for garnish

⅓ cup chopped toasted mixed nuts and seeds, such as almonds, walnuts, peanuts, pumpkin seeds, and/or sunflower seeds, for garnish

Lemon wedges, for garnish

• Heat 1 tablespoon of the oil in a deep, wide skillet or saucepan over medium-high heat. Add the quinoa and cook, stirring frequently, for 8 to 10 minutes, until the pan is dry and the quinoa has darkened a shade. Pour in the water. Bring to a boil, cover the pan, then reduce the heat to low and cook for 18 to 20 minutes, until the water is absorbed and the quinoa is fluffy. Remove from the heat and let stand for 10 minutes, or until ready to serve.

• Meanwhile, roll up the kale leaves, stems and all, and slice them into very thin ribbons, then place in a big mixing bowl. Mince together the ginger, garlic, and salt, smashing it with the flat side of the knife, scraping it up, and chopping it again, until the mixture resembles a paste. (You can also pound this mixture to a paste using a mortar and pestle.) Add to the kale. Using your hands, "massage" the kale, grabbing it in fistfuls and rubbing it gently until it softens, reduces in volume, and begins to exude liquid. Pour out the liquid. Stir in the remaining 2 tablespoons olive oil.

• Cook the dumplings as directed in the individual recipes.

• Divide the quinoa among four bowls, then divide the kale on top. Arrange 6 dumplings in each bowl. Garnish each serving with the herbs, nuts, and a lemon wedge. Serve immediately.

basics and components

The "component cooking" style used in this book is about combining a few little things—some marinated greens, a fried egg, a little scoop of kimchi, a pile of freshly cooked noodles or grains, and perhaps a few ladlefuls of flavorful broth—in a bowl to make something that's more than the sum of its parts. This isn't so different from the more familiar, "protein-side-side" style—you must cook each of those components separately too; you just aren't encouraged to eat them all in the same bite.

I don't want to scare you, but there's no way around this: The secret to delicious but effortless weeknight cooking is to plan ahead. The better equipped your pantry and refrigerator, the more easy options you'll have at your fingertips when you want a great, quick meal. And this includes prep work. Thinking of recipes like a restaurant prep cook—that is, breaking them down into parts that can be divvied up—is the way to get ahead. Vegetarian cooking requires lots of cleaning, peeling, slicing, and dicing vegetables. So, for example, getting into the habit of washing your vegetables right when you bring them home eliminates a hurdle come dinnertime. The idea is to do your future self some favors.

Included in this chapter are some of the foundations of the recipes in *Bowl*, like dashi, pho broth, and rice cooking methods. There are some easy ways to streamline these processes. Get kombu soaking in the morning, and you'll have dashi ready when you get home from work. The work of preparing brown rice, which cooks more quickly and more nutritionally after it's had some time to soak, can similarly be split into parts. Pho broth and vegetable stock are excellent weekend projects: Once cooled, divide into freezer-safe, one-pint containers—each of which is roughly a single portion—and freeze for future, easy weeknight use. Boil a half-dozen eggs at once; you can rewarm them in a bowl of hot tap water. The Rayu, Chili Oil, and Togarashi Blend are enhancements, which can often be swapped with a store-bought substitution—but they're good, fun, and easy projects that are perfect to make when you have a bit of extra time to spare.

If you're an experienced cook, you may already have your own ways of doing the kinds of things covered in this chapter. If not, start here and incorporate these methods into your regular cooking so that they become second nature. Over time you may find that you prefer a more strongly flavored dashi, so you'll opt to use more kombu than I call for. And assuming you do take to dashi, you'll use the opportunity to try out a few different brands of kombu and find your favorite. Maybe you'll prefer to use a light-flavored, store-bought vegetable stock, but brighten it up with a few herbs, garlic, and ginger. These are the kinds of discoveries and rewards that await you, and are how my recipes will become yours.

vegetarian dashi

The first time I made dashi I was shocked by how easy it was. Just cover kombu with water, and let it sit. That's it. No chopping, no simmering, no skimming, and usually no straining. Traditionally the liquid is steeped with bonito flakes, but since bonito is made from dried fish, it's omitted here. Dried shiitake mushrooms add flavor instead. But even without the bonito flakes, dashi is surprisingly rich in umami, in part because kombu contains some of the same naturally occurring glutamates that appear in MSG. I've included both cold and hot water methods—the cold water method produces a better-tasting dashi, with a fuller flavor, but when you haven't been able to plan ahead, the hot water method will work fine. After you get into the habit, you might do as I do and reserve a big Mason jar specifically for dashi. MAKES 2 QUARTS

Four 2-inch squares kombu (about 1½ ounces)   2 quarts cold water
4 dried shiitake mushrooms

• Combine the kombu, mushrooms, and water in a large container and let stand for at least 30 minutes, or up to 12 hours. It gets stronger as it sits, and the taste can vary depending on what type of kombu you use, so with a few rounds you'll find your preference. If you plan to let it stand for more than 4 hours, place it in the refrigerator, lidded or covered with a piece of plastic wrap.

• Alternatively, bring the water to a bare simmer in a saucepan. Remove from the heat, add the kombu and mushrooms, and let stand for 30 minutes.

• Discard the kombu. Pick out the mushrooms and trim off and discard the stems. Reserve the mushroom caps for another use. You may want to strain the dashi through a fine-mesh sieve or cheesecloth if there are small pieces of kombu left behind, but I rarely do this.

• Stored in an airtight container, the dashi will keep for 2 or 3 days.

VARIATION For a richer dashi, substitute unsalted Asian-Style Vegetable Stock (page 219) for the water in the hot-water method above.

vegetarian pho broth

Like ramen, traditional versions of pho broth rely on meat for richness, body, and flavor. Vegetarian adaptations are a more delicate affair, and the bright herbs, warm spices, and sweetness of the vegetables must shine in balance. Blackening the ginger and onion is a standard step, lending depth and astringency, and you shouldn't skip it. This recipe makes a satisfying stand-alone broth that has the power to nourish and rejuvenate. After an hour of simmering, most any vegetable will have given up all of its flavor to the liquid, and some will even turn bitter if you continue cooking them for too long. I hold off seasoning this broth with salt and sugar until just before serving. This recipe makes enough for two 4-serving batches of pho. MAKES ABOUT 3 QUARTS

1 large or 2 small onions, peeled and quartered lengthwise

2 ounces fresh ginger (a 3- to 4-inch piece, depending on thickness)

2 tablespoons peanut oil

2 medium leeks, white and green parts, coarsely chopped into 1-inch pieces

2 large carrots, coarsely chopped into 1-inch pieces

1 medium daikon radish (12 ounces), peeled and coarsely chopped into 1-inch pieces

10 garlic cloves, peeled

1 stalk fresh lemongrass, smashed and coarsely chopped

3 whole star anise

3 whole cloves

2 cinnamon sticks

½ teaspoon fennel seeds

5 dried shiitake mushrooms

Small handful of fresh cilantro stems

• Preheat the broiler. Arrange the onions and ginger on a foil-lined baking sheet. Once the broiler is hot, broil the vegetables close to the heat source until charred all over, flipping them with tongs as needed. Remove the onions if they cook more quickly than the ginger, or vice versa.

• Alternatively, char the onions and ginger over the open flame of a gas burner, turning them periodically, until blackened all over. This will need to be done in a few batches.

(*continued* on page 218)

shortcut pho broth

This version of pho broth saves some time with chopping and sourcing vegetables, and can be a great way to use up any lingering containers of vegetable stock in your freezer. If you're in a pinch, you can skip the step of blackening the ginger; instead, slice it into thin coins and add it to the vegetable stock along with the other aromatics. MAKES ABOUT 1¾ QUARTS

1 ounce fresh ginger (2 thumb-sized pieces)

2 quarts Asian-Style Vegetable Stock (page 219) or store-bought low-sodium vegetable broth

3 garlic cloves, peeled

2 whole star anise

2 whole cloves

1 cinnamon stick

1 stalk fresh lemongrass, smashed and coarsely chopped, or 1½ teaspoons dried

Small handful of fresh cilantro stems

• Turn a gas burner on high. Using heat-safe tongs, hold the ginger over the flame and turn it as needed until charred all over. This will take 5 to 7 minutes. Alternatively, if you don't have a gas range, blacken the ginger in the broiler, as directed in the recipe opposite.

• In a saucepan, combine the vegetable stock with the blackened ginger, garlic, star anise, cloves, cinnamon, and lemongrass. Bring to a boil, then reduce to a simmer and cook for 25 to 35 minutes, until the aromatics begin to shine through in the flavor. Add the cilantro stems and simmer for another 5 minutes.

• Strain the broth through a cheesecloth-lined sieve, gathering up the ends of the cheesecloth so as to squeeze out as much liquid as possible. Once completely cooled, pack it in containers, and store in the refrigerator for up to 1 day or in the freezer for up to 2 months for future use.

• Heat the oil in a stockpot over medium-high heat. Once hot, add the leeks, carrots, daikon, garlic, lemongrass, star anise, cloves, cinnamon, and fennel seeds. Stir to coat in the oil, then cover and cook for 5 minutes, until fragrant and the colors of the vegetables are vibrant. Coarsely chop the charred ginger, then add it, the onions, and the mushrooms to the pot and cover with cold water; you'll need about 4 quarts. Bring to a boil, then reduce to a gentle simmer and cook for 1 hour, at which point the broth should be strongly flavored. Add the cilantro stems and cook for another 5 minutes.

• Strain the broth through a cheesecloth-lined sieve, in batches as necessary, gathering up the ends of the cheesecloth so as to squeeze out as much liquid as possible. Once completely cooled, pack in containers and store in the refrigerator for up to 1 day or in the freezer for up to 2 months.

asian-style vegetable stock

This excellent stock has a few important layers of flavor to give it depth and body. Dried shiitakes are soaked and the softened stems, as well as the flavorful soaking liquid, are added to the pot. Then a host of common Asian vegetables are sautéed in toasted sesame oil to coax out the natural juices and caramelize slightly to establish a rich base. Following that, I use a trick I learned in a kimchi-making class at the Purple Yam restaurant in Brooklyn several years ago: The stock is removed from the heat and steeped with a piece of kombu, which infuses the stock with saline depth. This stock freezes very well. MAKES ABOUT 2 QUARTS

8 dried shiitake mushrooms, preferably ones that contain the stems

1½ cups hot water, plus 10 cups water for the stock

1 small or ½ large daikon radish (about 1 pound), peeled and top trimmed off

1 large carrot (about 8 ounces)

1 leek (washed) or onion, root end trimmed

1½ ounces ginger (3 thumb-sized pieces)

5 plump garlic cloves

1 bunch scallions

2 tablespoons toasted sesame oil

Two 2-inch squares kombu

• Cover the dried mushrooms with the 1½ cups hot water in a bowl. Let stand for 20 to 30 minutes, until completely soft. Remove the mushrooms and separate the stems from the caps. Reserve the caps for another use and set the stems aside. Strain the liquid through a coffee filter into a small bowl or measuring cup and set aside.

• While the mushrooms are reconstituting, prepare the vegetables: Halve the daikon, carrot, and leek lengthwise and then chop into 3- to 4-inch lengths. Chop the ginger on the bias into ½-inch slabs. Smash the garlic and remove most of the skin. Cut the scallions into 2-inch lengths.

• Heat a stockpot over medium heat and add the oil. Once hot, add the prepared vegetables and the reserved mushroom stems. Toss the vegetables in the oil, then cover the pot and cook for 5 minutes, until fragrant and the vegetables are vibrant. Pour in the 10 cups water and increase the heat to high. Just as the water comes to a boil, reduce the heat and simmer, uncovered, for 25 minutes. Pour in the reserved mushroom soaking liquid.

• Remove the stock from the heat and add the kombu. Let cool completely.

• Strain the stock through a cheesecloth-lined sieve, gathering up the ends of the cheesecloth so as to squeeze out as much liquid as possible. At this point you can pack the stock in containers and store it in the refrigerator for 2 days or in the freezer for up to 2 months.

flame tamer

The stovetop in my apartment runs very hot compared to most others that I've cooked on, so one of my first purchases was a flame tamer, which helps to control the heat on low settings, as for rice. A flame tamer is simply a heavy disk, usually made from cast-iron, that sits directly on top of the burner and acts as a buffer and even distributor of the heat. It works terrifically at regulating the heat for dishes like stovetop rice.

stovetop steamed white rice

Many cooks feel anxious about cooking rice on a stovetop. I think that part of this is due to the misconception that you can't check on rice as it's cooking. While it's not ideal to let all of the steam escape while removing the lid, it's not true that you can't peek in on rice's progress, particularly toward the end of the cooking. And in my experience, the popularly used proportion of one part rice to two parts water is too much water, and usually leads to a wet mess. You can always add another few teaspoons of water if the rice is dry when you check, but there's not much that can be done if the rice is overcooked. I am a big fan of my rice cooker, which eliminates this anxiety altogether. VARIABLE YIELD

for 2 servings
1 cup medium- or long-grain white rice

1½ cups water, plus more for rinsing

for 4 or 5 servings
2 cups medium- or long-grain white rice

3 cups water, plus more for rinsing

• Put the rice in a small or medium saucepan, depending on the yield, and cover with water to rinse. Swish the grains vigorously with your fingers to remove excess starch, then drain thoroughly in a sieve. Return the rice to the saucepan and cover with the measured water.

• Place over high heat and bring the liquid to a full boil. Cover the pot, reduce the heat to the lowest setting—place the pot on a flame tamer if your stove is hot (see box, opposite)—and cook, covered, for 15 to 18 minutes, until the water is absorbed and the grains are tender but not mushy or overcooked. Remove from the heat, fluff with a fork, and let stand for at least 10 minutes, covered, before serving.

stovetop brown rice

Brown rice takes more than twice as long to cook as white, but the process can be hastened a bit by letting the grains soak for a few hours first. I'll usually leave it to soak before I head out in the morning, so that it's ready to be cooked when I get home at night. But even 2 hours of soaking is feasible if you tend to eat late, as I do. Steaming brown rice, following the absorption method used for white rice, is tricky. Instead, the following method for boiling brown rice produces consistent results, allowing quite a lot of control as well as a faster cooking time.

VARIABLE YIELD

for 2 servings
1 cup long- or medium-grain brown rice

for 4 or 5 servings
2½ cups long- or medium-grain brown rice

• Place the rice in a bowl and cover with water. Swish the grains between your fingers and pick out any bits of debris, then drain.

• To presoak the rice, cover with at least 3 inches of water and let stand for at least 2 hours, or up to 8 hours. Drain.

• Combine the rice and at least 3 quarts of water in a large saucepan. Place over high heat and bring to a boil. Continue boiling until the rice is almost cooked—the grains should be chewy, with just a tiny bit of crunch left in them, 15 to 18 minutes for soaked rice, 20 to 25 for unsoaked. Reserve a ladleful of the cooking water, then drain the rice through a sieve.

• Immediately return the rice to the pot and add 2 tablespoons of the reserved cooking water. Reduce the heat to low, place the pot over the heat, and steam, covered, for about 5 minutes more, until the water is absorbed and the rice is tender. Remove from the heat, fluff with a fork, and let stand for at least 10 minutes, covered, before serving.

mixed grains

This approach to mixing grains was a happy accident that occured when I was short on rice and made up for the shortage with quinoa, which has the same cooking time. This is a great way to add some complexity of flavor and texture to white rice, as well as some protein, since both quinoa and millet are good sources of it. These mixed grains can be used interchangeably in the recipes for bibimbap and other grain bowls, and are even good in the recipes for fried rice. If you want to use brown rice here instead of white, it unfortunately doesn't work as a streamlined, one-pot method, but it's easy enough to just mix cooked brown rice together with the cooked quinoa-millet. MAKES ABOUT 4½ CUPS

2/3 cup medium-grain white rice

2/3 cup quinoa

2/3 cup millet

3½ cups water, plus more for rinsing

1 tablespoon toasted sesame seeds (optional)

• Put the rice, quinoa, and millet in a medium saucepan and cover with water to rinse. Swish the grains vigorously with your fingers, then drain thoroughly in a sieve. Return the grains to the saucepan and cover with the 3½ cups water.

• Place over high heat and bring the liquid to a full boil. Cover the pot, reduce the heat to the lowest setting—place the pot on a flame tamer if your stove is hot (see page 220)—and cook for 15 to 18 minutes, until the water is absorbed and the grains are tender but not mushy or overcooked. Remove from the heat, fluff with a fork, and fold in the sesame seeds, if using. Let stand for at least 10 minutes, covered, before serving.

boiled eggs

Boiled eggs are terrific in ramen and many other bowls, and are handy for planning meals in advance. A cooked, boiled egg can sit in the fridge for several days, still in its shell, and molten-yolk eggs can be rewarmed in a bowl of hot tap water before serving. These instructions offer you either a molten yolk or a firm one. Molten yolks, which are still a bit liquid, enrich the body and flavor of brothy bowls; firm-cooked eggs are great chopped up in grain salads or packed up for meals on the go. But if you have salmonella concerns, be sure to cook the yolk until it's firm. VARIABLE YIELD

Salt

Large eggs, in their shells, ideally at room temperature

• Prepare an ice-water bath.

• Bring a saucepan of water to boil, and salt it generously. Using a spider skimmer or slotted spoon, lower the eggs—as many as you'd like to cook, or as many as can fit comfortably in a single layer—into the water, ensuring that they're fully submerged. Stir the eggs periodically to keep the yolks centered.

• **For a molten yolk:** Lower the heat to maintain a gentle boil and cook the eggs for 7 minutes.

• **For a firm yolk:** Remove the pan from the heat, cover it, and let the eggs stand for 11 minutes.

• Lift the eggs out of the water with the spider skimmer and plunge into the ice bath to cool.

• To peel the eggs, crack all over, then peel back the skin while holding the egg in the ice water or under cold running water.

fried eggs

The whites of an egg consist of two parts, the more viscous inner albumen, and the thinner outer one. The thinner, outer albumen is what spreads unattractively when you crack the egg into the pan. If you want to make an especially photogenic fried egg—one that's more evenly round and plump—the outer albumen can be strained off by cracking the egg into a small sieve and gently shaking it until it runs off. Eggs fried gently over low heat will have a soft, delicate texture, and eggs cooked over higher heat will develop a crispy, frilly edge that's appealing. Instructions for both are included here. MAKES 1 TO 3 EGGS

Neutral-tasting oil

Large eggs

Salt

½ teaspoon water or soy sauce per egg

• **For soft-fried eggs:** Heat a skillet over low heat (if your burner runs hot, set the skillet over a flame tamer, see page 220). A small, 6-inch skillet will only fit one egg; larger 12- to 15-inch skillets will fit up to three. Add enough oil to coat the base of the skillet. Once hot, crack in the eggs and sprinkle with salt. Cook for 60 to 90 seconds, until the whites appear set. Sprinkle water or, if desired, soy sauce over the eggs, cover, and cook for another 1 to 3 minutes, until the whites are set and the yolks are cooked to your liking.

• **For crispy-fried eggs:** Heat a skillet over medium-high heat. A small, 6-inch skillet will only fit one egg; larger 12- to 15-inch skillets will fit up to three. Add enough oil to liberally coat the base of the skillet. Once hot, crack in the eggs and sprinkle with salt. Lower the heat to medium-low. Use a paring knife to pop any bubbles that develop, and cook for about 60 seconds, tilting the pan back and forth a bit so that some of the excess oil runs over the tops of the eggs, until the whites are mostly set. Sprinkle water or, if desired, soy sauce over the eggs, cover the skillet, and cook for another 30 to 60 seconds, until the whites are set and the yolks are cooked to your liking.

poached eggs

Poaching eggs is a wonderful skill to master. They can be substituted for fried or soft-yolk boiled eggs as you wish. I find that the trick is to get the water heated up correctly—a full boil will break up the egg, but too gentle a simmer and the egg sinks to the bottom and flattens out; the goal is an "aggressive simmer." If cooking more than 1 egg, keep the cooked eggs in a bowl of tepid water as you continue poaching, then rewarm them by dipping them into the simmering poaching water just before serving. MAKES 1 EGG

3 tablespoons white vinegar

Fine sea salt

1 large egg

• Bring a small saucepan of water to a boil. And the vinegar and salt the poaching liquid generously. Reduce the heat so as to maintain a gentle but steady boil.

• Crack the egg into a small bowl. With a spider skimmer or slotted spoon, stir the water until you get a whirlpool going. Pour the egg directly into the vortex. Use the spoon to keep the water circulating around the egg (I find that this helps with the shape, and keeps the egg from sinking to the bottom of the pan as the water comes back to temperature). Cook, stirring gently and more or less constantly, for about 2 minutes.

• Use the slotted spoon to lift the egg out of the water. Touch it gently with your finger or a spoon to test the progress of the cooking. Eventually you'll learn to know by touch when the egg is done to your liking. A runny yolk usually takes 2 to 2½ minutes; a molten one between 3 and 3½, and a firm yolk will take about 4 minutes.

• Remove from the water with the skimmer or spoon and gently blot dry on a clean kitchen towel, then serve.

napa cabbage or bok choy kimchi

Most traditional kimchi is made with fish sauce or some form of salted shrimp, or both. Vegetarian versions are a little lighter and brighter, drawing more flavors from fermentation, garlic, and ginger. While this one is very garlicky and gingery, it has a clean finish that I find irresistible. The trick is to get the salt and sugar right—taste carefully before you pack it up. And good salt makes a difference. One of my favorite ways to eat it is with a fork, right out of the jar. MAKES ABOUT 1 QUART

2 pounds Napa cabbage or mature bok choy

¼ cup kosher salt, plus more as needed

3 tablespoons sweet (glutinous) rice flour or all-purpose flour

1 bunch watercress, tough stems discarded, torn into bite-sized pieces

4 thin scallions, trimmed and cut into 2-inch segments

1 heaping tablespoon minced fresh ginger

1 heaping tablespoon minced garlic

3 tablespoons Korean pepper flakes, plus more as needed (see note on page 228 for a substitute)

1 tablespoon brown sugar, plus more as needed

1 teaspoon good-quality, textured salt, like fleur de sel or sel gris, plus more as needed

• If using cabbage, discard any limp or discolored outer leaves. Quarter it lengthwise, so that you have 4 wedges, then trim out the core. Cut each quarter into thirds so that you have lots of long strips. If using bok choy, trim the leaves off the core and separate the leaves from the thick white stems. Cut the stems into 1½- to 2-inch segments. Wash thoroughly, swishing in a large bowl of water. Cut the leaves into halves or thirds, depending on their size.

• Place the cabbage or bok choy in a large mixing bowl or food-grade bucket that can comfortably fit it. Stir ¼ cup kosher salt into 4 quarts of water in a large pitcher with a slotted spoon until dissolved. Taste the brine—it must be well seasoned, as salty as, if not a touch saltier than, seawater. Stir in additional salt or water as needed. Pour the brine over the vegetables. If it isn't enough to cover them completely, prepare more brine, 1 tablespoon salt to 1 quart of water. Weigh down the vegetables with a plate so that they are fully submerged. Leave out at room temperature for 24 hours. Drain, gently pressing on the vegetables to extract liquid. Place in a large mixing bowl.

- Meanwhile, whisk together the flour with ¾ cup water in a small saucepan. Place over medium heat and, whisking constantly, cook until thickened to the consistency of glue. This will happen quickly, in about 2 minutes. Remove from the heat and cool completely. This mixture can be made up to a day ahead and stored in an airtight container in the refrigerator.

- Add the remaining ingredients to the cabbage or bok choy. Add about half of the flour paste and, using gloved hands, mix well, making sure to coat the vegetables thoroughly. The kimchi should be thoroughly moistened; if it seems dry, add additional flour paste as needed. Taste the kimchi: as it ferments, it will develop a lot of funky flavor, but at this point you should taste for balance of salt, sugar, and heat, and adjust as necessary.

- Pack the kimchi into glass pint or quart jars, making sure to evenly distribute the watercress and scallions and leaving at least ¾ inch headspace. Wipe the rims clean and seal tightly. Put the jars on a baking sheet, which will catch any juices that might bubble out of the jars, and leave out for 48 hours at room temperature. Move to the refrigerator. The kimchi will generate more liquid and the cabbage will collapse in the jars. Turn them upside down periodically to redistribute the liquid, and open them every few days to release some of the gas pressure inside.

- The kimchi is safe to eat at any point, but it's best after at least a week of fermenting. It will keep for at least a month, and often much longer.

korean red pepper flakes

Korean red pepper flakes—called *gochugaru*—can be hard to find except at well-stocked Asian and Korean markets. *Gochugaru*, light and flaky in texture, is sold in large bags, and—check the ingredients—sometimes has added salt. (Try to find one that does not have added salt.) Most importantly, it's very mild because it doesn't contain the seeds of the pepper. You can substitute about ½ teaspoon crushed red pepper flakes in this recipe, along with a pinch or two of smoked paprika, which adds some complexity to the heat. The results won't be the same, but they'll still be very good.

pickled red onions

Pickled onions perk up anything they're added to: all manner of green and grain salads, omelets, sandwiches, burgers, tacos, even a bowl of beans. This recipe makes pickled onions that have a good balance of salty, slightly sweet, and sharp taste and tenderness, without any raw bite left in them. One way to play around here is to throw in some spices or other aromatics—try crushed coriander, star anise, bay leaves, dried chilies, cloves, peppercorns, cloves of garlic, or slices of ginger. MAKES 1 HEAPING CUP

1 large red onion

⅓ cup white vinegar

⅓ cup rice vinegar

⅓ cup water

1½ teaspoons sugar

½ teaspoon fine sea salt

• Peel the onion, then slice it into rings ⅛ inch wide or thinner using a mandoline or a sharp chef's knife and a steady hand.

• Combine the white and rice vinegars, water, sugar, and salt in a small saucepan. Bring to a boil, then add the onions. Gently stir the onions until they soften and are submerged in the brine; this will take 1 to 2 minutes. Remove from the heat and let cool completely. Transfer to an airtight container and store in the refrigerator, where they'll keep for several weeks.

quick cucumber pickles

I've loved cucumbers all my life, and have always preferred the fresh flavor and crunch of quick-pickled ones to the less snappy and often rubbery ones that emerge from brines. In bowls, quick pickles provide contrast in the form of coolness and some zingy crunch, and this easy method makes a clean, straight-forward quick pickle. Salting seasons and softens their texture, and tossing them with vinegar adds the necessary acid, but without the waste of a brine. MAKES ABOUT 2 CUPS

4 small firm cucumbers, such as Kirby or Persian

1 tablespoon sugar

1½ teaspoons fine sea salt

1 tablespoon rice vinegar

• If desired, peel the cucumbers. If not peeling, scrub the peels thoroughly. Slice the cucumbers into ⅛-inch-thick rounds (or thinner if desired) using a mandoline or a sharp knife. Toss with the sugar and salt and leave in a colander to drain for 20 to 30 minutes. Rinse well and drain. In a bowl, toss with the vinegar, tasting and adding more as desired. Stored in an airtight container in the refrigerator, these pickles will keep for up to 1 week.

ramen noodles (traditional)

What distinguishes Japanese and Chinese wheat noodles from their similar-looking Italian counterparts is the use of alkali. Some 2,000 years ago, mineral- and alkali-rich well water was used for noodles, but now these types of noodles are made with a concentrated liquid called *kansui* (Japan), or the dry chemical compounds sodium bicarbonate and potassium carbonate, which are what make up the liquid concentrate. The purpose is to give the noodles a firm but buoyant structure, a distinctive but subtle toasty flavor, and their trademark yellow color. *Kansui* can be found at most Japanese markets and ordered online, and once you get your hands on it, it's surprisingly easy to make good, authentic ramen noodles at home. MAKES 4 SERVINGS

2 cups bread flour, or 2 cups all-purpose flour plus 2 teaspoons vital wheat gluten

1/2 cup warm water

2 teaspoons *kansui* (see above and Sources, page 249)

Cornstarch, for dusting

• Place the flour in the bowl of a stand mixer fitted with the paddle attachment or a food processor fitted with the dough blade. Stir together the water and *kansui* in a small bowl or liquid measuring cup, then pour into the flour. Stir until combined, or pulse several times in the food processor. The mixture will be crumbly. If using a stand mixer, gather the crumbles into a ball and knead for a few moments; return to the mixing bowl, switch to the dough hook, and knead for about 5 minutes, until the flour has absorbed all of the liquid and you have a cohesive, slightly shaggy-looking ball. If using a food processor, continue to pulse the dough until it coheres into a slightly shaggy-looking ball, then transfer to a work surface and knead for 1 to 2 minutes. You should be able to shape it into a ball without it crumbling apart. You can add additional water by the teaspoon if the dough is too crumbly, but be aware that this is a dense and dry dough. If it is too wet, the finished pasta will lack its distinguishing chew.

• Shape the dough into a ball, wrap with plastic, and let rest for 30 minutes.

• Divide the dough into quarters. Clear away the necessary space to work. Work with one quarter at a time and keep the remaining dough covered with plastic to prevent drying. Flatten the dough into a rectangle, dust with cornstarch, and roll through a pasta machine on its widest setting. Fold the sheet in half, flatten it out, and repeat. Do this once more. Reduce the thickness setting by one notch and pass the dough through the machine. Repeat this process once, then reduce the setting again, pass the dough through, and repeat, all the while dusting the sheets lightly with cornstarch as you work if they start to get stuck. You'll want sheets slightly less than $\frac{1}{16}$ inch thick, which is typically the number 3 setting on a pasta machine. Dust lightly with cornstarch, fold the sheets up without creasing them, and keep covered with plastic to prevent drying out as you repeat with the remaining 3 quarters of dough.

• Pass a sheet through the pasta machine's spaghetti or linguini setting, trimming the noodles with scissors to make strands that are 10 to 12 inches long. Toss the noodles with cornstarch, then curl the strands loosely around your hand to make a nest. Cover with plastic and proceed with the remaining sheets.

• If not using immediately, store the noodles in resealable bags in the refrigerator or freezer. In the refrigerator they'll keep for 1 to 2 days; in the freezer they'll keep for about 2 months.

• To cook the noodles, bring a pot of water to a rapid boil. Cook for 60 to 90 seconds, using a strainer basket or the pasta insert that comes with your stockpot, if you have one, until just tender. Pull the noodles from the cooking water and rinse under cold running water to remove excess starch. Dip back into the reserved cooking water to rewarm, then divide among four bowls and serve, topped as directed in the individual recipes.

VARIATION You can use between a quarter and a third whole-wheat or other whole-grain flour. You will need to add additional water as the dough is mixing, since whole-grain flours absorb more of it. The finished noodles will be more chewy and less stretchy, but the added flavor is sometimes a worthwhile sacrifice.

ramen noodles (nontraditional)

Traditional ramen noodles (page 232) are very good if you're up for an experiment. But if you're unable or unwilling to track down the *kansui*, this is the recipe I developed first, based loosely on the one for homemade ramen noodles in Nancy Singleton Hachisu's wonderful book *Japanese Farm Food*. There's some disagreement on whether or not ramen noodles should contain egg—many store-bought dried and fresh noodles destined for ramen do, while alkaline-style noodle recipes typically do not—but the egg in these noodles makes the dough much easier to work with. These are very good, very versatile noodles, richer in flavor and chewier in texture than standard wheat noodles used traditionally in ramen. I like the addition of some whole-grain flour, which significantly deepens the flavor. MAKES 4 SERVINGS

1½ cups bread flour, or 1½ cups all-purpose flour plus 2 teaspoons vital wheat gluten

½ cup whole-wheat flour

2 teaspoons baking soda

1 tablespoon neutral-tasting oil

1 egg

1 large egg yolk

2 tablespoons water

Cornstarch, for dusting

• Combine the bread and whole-wheat flours and baking soda in the bowl of a stand mixer fitted with the paddle attachment, or in the bowl of a food processor fitted with the dough blade. Add the oil and stir or pulse until crumbly. In a small bowl, lightly whisk together the egg, yolk, and water, then pour into the flour mixture. If using a stand mixer, gather the crumbles into a ball and knead for a few moments; return to the mixing bowl, switch to the dough hook, and knead for about 5 minutes, until the flour has absorbed all of the liquid and you have a cohesive, slightly shaggy-looking ball. If using a food processor, continue to pulse the dough until it coheres into a slightly shaggy-looking ball, then transfer to a work surface and knead for 1 to 2 minutes. You should be able to shape it into a ball without it crumbling apart. You can add additional water by the teaspoon, but be aware that this is a dry, leathery dough.

• Shape the dough into a ball, wrap with plastic, and let rest for 30 minutes.

• Divide the dough into quarters. Clear away the necessary space to work. Work with one quarter at a time and keep the remaining dough covered with plastic to prevent drying. Flatten the dough into a rectangle, dust with cornstarch, and roll through a pasta machine on its widest setting. Fold the sheet in half, flatten it out, and repeat. Do this once more. Reduce the thickness setting by one notch and pass the dough through. Repeat this process once, then reduce the setting again, pass the dough through, and repeat, all the while dusting the sheets lightly with cornstarch as you work. You'll want sheets slightly less than $1/16$ inch thick, which is typically the number 3 setting on a pasta machine. Dust lightly with cornstarch, fold the sheets up without creasing them, and keep covered with plastic to prevent drying out as you repeat with the remaining 3 quarters of dough.

• Pass a sheet through the pasta machine's spaghetti or linguini setting, trimming the pasta with scissors to make strands that are about 12 inches long. Toss the noodles with cornstarch, then curl the strands loosely around your hand to make a nest. Cover with plastic and proceed with the remaining sheets.

• If not using immediately, store the noodles in resealable bags in the refrigerator or freezer. In the refrigerator they'll keep for 1 to 2 days; in the freezer they'll keep for about 2 months.

• To cook the noodles, bring a pot of water to a rapid boil. Add the noodles and cook for 60 to 90 seconds, until just tender. Fish out the noodles from the cooking water with a sieve and rinse under cold running water, to remove excess starch. Dip back into the reserved cooking water to rewarm, then divide among four bowls and serve, topped as directed in the individual recipes.

chili oil

There are lots of different ways to approach chili oil, and I've included three of them in this chapter (including Rayu, page 238, and Chili-Bean Oil, page 240). This first recipe is basic, and is the strongest argument I can make for not opting for a store-bought bottle. Chili oil adds a sometimes welcome kick to ramen and pho, as well as richness and body, and in this recipe, it's a flavor-forward dry heat. Any kind of crushed red peppers will work, but those purchased at a Chinese or Asian market are preferable. And the Sichuan peppercorns, which are very inexpensive at those markets, lend some of their cool, numbing properties to the oil. MAKES 1 CUP

1 cup neutral-tasting oil

¼ cup red pepper flakes

2 tablespoons Sichuan peppercorns (optional)

• Heat the oil in a small saucepan until shimmering but not smoking—the temperature should be about 350°F.

• Meanwhile, place the pepper flakes and peppercorns, if using, in a heat-safe jar or other container.

• Very carefully pour the hot oil into the jar. You should hear some sizzling and see some foaming on the surface. Let cool completely, then seal with a lid and let stand for 2 or 3 days for the flavors to develop before using. Kept in a cool, dry place, the chili oil will keep for up to 3 months.

rayu

A spoonful of this sweet, spicy seasoning oil goes a long way towards adding richness and spice to vegetarian ramen. (I also sometimes like it in pho.) Rayu is made many different ways in Japanese cuisine, from simple chili-infused oil to more complicated spice blends made with fresh and dried chilies, though typically it contains some toasted sesame oil. This one has lots of good texture, from bits of caramelized onion to nubby seeds and spices. Coriander seeds are unorthodox, but I love the slight fruitiness that they add. This rayu must be cooked in a saucepan, rather than a small skillet—the oil bubbles up dramatically as the water cooks out of the shallots and garlic. MAKES ABOUT ¾ CUP

½ cup neutral-tasting oil

½ cup finely minced shallots

2 heaping tablespoons minced garlic

1½ teaspoons fine sea salt

1 teaspoon sesame seeds

2 teaspoons toasted sesame oil

1 teaspoon crushed coriander seeds

½ teaspoon red pepper flakes

• Combine the neutral-tasting oil, shallots, garlic, salt, and sesame seeds in a small saucepan. Place over low heat and cook, stirring frequently, for 30 to 60 minutes, until the water cooks out of the vegetables and the shallot and garlic are richly golden brown. Remove from the heat, add the sesame oil, coriander, and red pepper flakes, and let cool completely. Stored in an airtight container at room temperature, the oil will keep for up to 2 months.

chili-bean oil

The inspiration for this recipe comes from Andrea Nguyen's always delightful and enlightening website *Viet World Kitchen*, and was originally published in Barbara Tropp's *China Moon Cookbook*. Fermented black beans are such a particular, umami-rich flavor, that this is the oil to use when you want to add something unexpected. MAKES A GENEROUS ½ CUP

2 tablespoons fermented black beans

3 tablespoons red pepper flakes

1 tablespoon grated fresh ginger

½ cup neutral-tasting oil

1 tablespoon toasted sesame oil

• Place the fermented black beans in a small bowl and cover with cold water. Let stand for 20 minutes, then drain and rinse. Blot dry with a paper towel, then coarsely chop.

• Combine the beans in a small skillet or saucepan with the red pepper flakes, ginger, and neutral-tasting and sesame oils, and place over medium-low heat. Once the oil starts sizzling, watch closely and adjust the heat as necessary to maintain a gentle simmer. Cook for 10 to 15 minutes, gently stirring periodically until the ginger is golden brown but not burnt, and some of the frothing has subsided.

• Remove from the heat and let cool completely. Transfer to a glass jar and store in a dry, cool space. The oil will keep for up to 2 months.

chili-garlic sambal

The red chilies needed to make this paste are usually available in the late summer and fall at farmers' markets. Look for red Thai chilies (Bird's eye chilies), and sometimes bins of serranos and jalapeños have red peppers hidden inside—they're just more mature, sun-ripened versions of their green counterparts. You want to use spicy rather than sweet ones in this sauce, and virtually any spicy red pepper you find can be used. Jarred *sambal oelek* uses white vinegar for flavor and as a preservative; the lime juice in this recipe imparts a bright, fresh flavor. This style of sambal is best enjoyed fresh, though it can be kept in the refrigerator for about a week. It can also be frozen, which is a great way to preserve its summery flavor for later in the year. MAKES ABOUT ½ CUP

5 ounces hot red chilies (see above)

3 garlic cloves, coarsely chopped

1 tablespoon sugar

½ teaspoon fine sea salt

1 tablespoon white vinegar

1 tablespoon lime juice

• Coarsely chop the chilies and trim out some or all of the seeds if desired (depending on how spicy you want the paste to be). Transfer to the bowl of a food processor or a mortar, and add the garlic, sugar, and salt. Pulse or pound with a pestle until a coarse paste forms.

• Transfer to a small saucepan, add the vinegar, and place over medium heat. Once the mixture begins simmering, cook for 5 to 7 minutes more, stirring periodically, until the raw edge has cooked off. Let cool, then stir in the lime juice. Taste and adjust the seasoning with more salt, sugar, or lime as needed, then store in an airtight container in the fridge for up to 1 week.

gochujang sauce

Gochujang has endless applications in marinades, dipping sauces, dressings, and spreads, and I always want it when I eat bibimbap. Asian markets and well-stocked supermarkets carry bottled *gochujang* sauces, but making your own is easy. This quick sauce serves to amplify the flavors of the *gochujang*, adding a bit more tang and sweetness. The other store-bought option is sriracha. MAKES ABOUT ½ CUP

¼ cup *gochujang* (see page 37)

1 tablespoon honey

2 teaspoons toasted sesame oil

1 tablespoon brown rice vinegar

1 to 2 tablespoons water

• Whisk together the *gochujang*, honey, oil, vinegar, and 1 tablespoon water. Add additional water to thin until you have a sauce that's a little bit thinner than glue. Stored in an airtight container in the refrigerator, the sauce will keep for at least 1 week.

garlic chips

Garlic chips are an excellent condiment for all types of soups and salads, but they're really good as a finishing touch for ramen and some pho. They add deep, assertive flavor as well as a bit of crunch. Cook them with care, because even a few seconds too long will make them too bitter to enjoy. And use them up within a day or so—their texture doesn't keep for much longer than that. Don't waste the oil—once it cools, strain it through cheesecloth, then use it for a future batch of garlic chips, or for pretty much any savory application. MAKES ABOUT ½ CUP

20 plump garlic cloves
Neutral-tasting oil

Fine sea salt

• Peel the garlic and then slice it very thinly. Pour about ½ inch of oil into a small skillet or saucepan over medium-low heat. Once hot, add the garlic. Adjust the heat as necessary to maintain a gentle simmer. Cook, stirring frequently, until the garlic is golden brown, which will take 5 to 15 minutes (the time varies depending on how thin you slice your garlic). It's important to watch closely and not let the chips burn.

• Use a spider skimmer or slotted spoon to transfer the garlic to a paper towel–lined plate. Sprinkle with a big pinch of salt and let cool completely. Stored in an airtight container at room temperature, they'll keep for 1 or 2 days.

frizzled shallots or scallions

Crispy, shallow-fried wisps of shallot or scallion are a perfect condiment to most any dish in this book, lending a burst of salty crunch. Since they don't retain their crispiness for more than a few hours, don't prepare them too far in advance. But if you make them the first step in your cooking, you'll be left with a shallot- or scallion-scented oil that can be strained and repurposed in other elements of the meal. Cutting the shallots into uniformly thin rings is important so that they all cook at the same rate. A mandoline is the tool to use. MAKES ABOUT ½ CUP

3 medium shallots, or ½ bunch scallions   Fine sea salt
Neutral-tasting oil

- If using shallots, peel, then slice into very thin rings using a mandoline.

- If using scallions, trim the ends off the scallions, then cut into 2- to 3-inch lengths. Cut each piece in half lengthwise. Lay the flat surface down on the cutting board and use a sharp knife to cut these segments into thin matchsticks.

- Heat ½ inch of oil in a small skillet or saucepan over medium heat. Test the temperature by adding a piece of shallot or scallion—it should sizzle on contact. Add the vegetables and cook, stirring frequently, until reddish brown all over, 6 to 12 minutes. Watch closely, as they can quickly burn toward the end.

- Use a spider skimmer or slotted spoon to transfer them to a paper towel–lined plate. Sprinkle with a pinch of salt and let cool completely. Use within a few hours.

- To save and repurpose the oil, strain it into a clean container through a few layers of cheese-cloth to catch any solids. The oil can be kept for up to 1 week.

togarashi blend

Togarashi, which translates as "Japanese chili pepper," is commonly available as spice blends like *shimi togarashi* and *nanami togarashi*. Ramen shops usually have vial-like containers of them at the table, and they're also easy to find at Japanese markets. Most recipes contain dried chilies, peppercorns, sesame seeds, and nori, as well as a number of variable items; the umami flavor of the nori is the standout. I keep a store-bought bottle on hand, but it's just as easy to make it, and a fresh homemade batch showcases the citrus zest. It's a wonderful thing for dishes that need a kick—I love it on avocado toast and hard-boiled eggs. Experiment with the zest; grapefruit is a great alternative to orange. MAKES ABOUT ¼ CUP

Three 2-inch squares toasted nori

1½ tablespoons toasted sesame seeds

1½ teaspoons dried orange or tangerine zest (see page 246)

1 teaspoon coarsely ground black pepper

1 teaspoon red pepper flakes

¾ teaspoon dried minced garlic

• Wave the nori square over the flame of a gas burner a few times, until the corners curl and they turn crisp, or roast under a broiler, flipping periodically. Break up into small pieces and add to a spice grinder or mortar along with half the sesame seeds, the citrus zest, black pepper, red pepper flakes, and garlic. Pulse or pound with a pestle until a coarse, dry mixture forms, then stir in the remaining sesame seeds. Stored in an airtight container at room temperature, the toragashi will keep for at least 1 month.

dried citrus zest

It's simple to dry your own citrus zest, and its flavor is so much more vibrant than store-bought that I've never purchased it from the spice aisle of the grocery store. This makes a pronounced difference in homemade togarashi, and also allows you to experiment with the zest. You'll want to use organic citrus here. VARIABLE YIELD

Oranges, lemons, grapefruit, or other citrus fruits

• Preheat an oven or toaster oven to 225°F. Line a baking sheet with parchment paper. Wash the citrus well, scrubbing off any wax that might be on the skin. Pat dry.

• Use a microplane or other citrus zester to remove all the flavorful outer skin of the citrus. Alternatively, use a vegetable peeler to remove it in strips, then scrape off any white pith with a spoon or the back side of a paring knife.

• Arrange the zest on the prepared baking sheet and bake for 15 to 30 minutes, until crisp and completely dry. The thick strips will take longer then the grated zest. Cool, then crumble the grated zest by folding the parchment over the top and rubbing with your fingers. Use a spice grinder or mortar and pestle to grind the strips. Store in an airtight container or resealable bag in the refrigerator, where it will keep for about 2 weeks. It loses its punch over time.

• One lemon yields about 1¼ teaspoons dried zest, 1 orange about 2 teaspoons, and 1 grapefruit about 1 tablespoon.

pounded ginger pulp

This great, simple condiment, which I read about in Naomi Duguid and Jeffrey Alford's transporting book *Hot Sour Salty Sweet*, adds a fresh, flowery punch to pho. Pounding fresh ginger with a bit of salt changes its flavor profile slightly, softening the sharpness a bit. Use ginger pulp in almost every kind of savory, broth-based soup, especially those meant to ward off sickness. You can also add it to a dressing or dipping sauce. It loses its pungency quickly, so you'll want to make this to order. MAKES 2 SCANT TABLESPOONS, ENOUGH FOR 4 SERVINGS

2 tablespoons coarsely chopped peeled fresh ginger

¼ teaspoon coarse salt

• Combine the ginger and salt in a mortar. Gently pound the mixture with a pestle until very moist and pureed and heady with fragrance.

• Alternatively, place the ginger in the center of a wide cutting board and sprinkle with the salt. Mince the mixture a few times, then flatten it out by pressing down and away with the broad side of a chef's knife, such that it spreads into a thin layer on the cutting board. Continue doing this until you have a moist paste.

sources

MISO PASTE

Miso Master
www.great-eastern-sun.com
Organic American-made miso paste

South River Miso Company
www.southrivermiso.com
Organic American-made small-batch miso
pastes

NOODLES

Sun Noodle
www.sunnoodle.com
Fresh ramen noodles

Lotus Foods
www.lotusfoods.com
Organic heritage rice noodles

Sobaya
www.sobaya.ca
Organic soba and other Japanese-style
noodles

King Soba
www.kingsoba.com
Organic and gluten-free noodles

Star Anise Foods
www.staranisefoods.com
Brown rice noodles and other gluten-free
noodles

RICE

Lotus Foods
www.lotusfoods.com
Organic heritage rice

Lundberg
www.lundberg.com
Organic rice

index